MW01172035

"Oh, Joy!" Copyrig Aiken, South Carolina. All rights reserved. Printed in the United States of America. No part of this publication may be reproduced, stored in a retrieval system or transmitted in any form or by any means without prior permission of the Author except in the case of brief quotations embodied in critical articles and reviews.

For more information, contact Cynthia Mitchell at joyfullpublishing@gmail.com.

Table of Contents

Foreword

Introduction

Foreword

OH, JOY!!! Finally, a member of the Body of Christ who is willing to be real. For too long Christian brothers and sisters have been silent about their salvation. I say often, if you have been saved at all, God has not only saved you from the penalty of sin and hell, but He has also saved you from the grip of sin, life's circumstances and situations. Yet, too many in the Body of Christ are ashamed or get amnesia when it comes to being thankful about the power of God's complete salvation.

Cynthia Mitchell's openness and honesty in this work are both inspiring and empowering. As she shares her story of brokenness, betrayal, rejection and disappointment, many will be able to identify with her struggles and her testimony. Yet, I praise God that this is not another tell-all book put forth to vent, blame or bash. She uses her pain as a means to learn the lessons of life that are teachable to others who may be suffering with similar life tragedies. It becomes clear to the reader that they, too, can learn from their pain and become "better" rather than "bitter."

While reading this book the one thing the reader is able to feel, even in the midst of Cynthia's pain, is her overwhelming sense of hope. This book is about believing, enduring and trusting God for a better day. In a time when people are suffering devastation from every facet of life, the one thing that people need to be reminded of is that they should never lose hope. Never give up. If one makes a decision that is proven to be the wrong decision, do not give up. Learn from it. Struggle not to repeat it. Yet, do not ever stop. There is a better day ahead.

Thank you, Cynthia. Thank you for your openness and transparency. Thank you for sharing your story and the lessons of your life with the world. Many will now know that they, too, can make it even in the midst of suffering, pain, divorce, disappointment and rejection. Many will now be blessed because you were not afraid or ashamed to be real with the world. Now many will know that they can and will be more than a conqueror if they will never lose heart. Keep the faith my sister, my daughter, my friend.

Dr. Gregory M. Fuller
Pastor, Macedonia Baptist Church

This writing is dedicated to my two precious gifts,
Cierra and Darius.
And to the memory of my Daddy,
the Reverend George Hayward Griffen.

Life can only be understood backward;

It must be lived forward.

~Soren Kierkegaad~

Introduction

It is my prayer that we, you and I, are in agreement right now. This is not a "tell all" book of secrets and dirty laundry. Some names have been changed for that very reason.

From beginning to end life is full of ups, downs situations and circumstances. Satan seeks every opportunity to kill our faith, steal our joy and keep us bound. Many mighty men and women of God stand on testimonies of overcoming family and generational strongholds that were manifested in molestation, major financial struggles, abandonment, mental illness and depression, alcohol, drug, sexual and other addictions. Affects such as patterns of wrong thinking, low self-esteem and inability to achieve, may be somewhat less noticeable but just as devastating. Although Satan will set up strongholds, we feed into his plans when we become too comfortable in captivity. We wear our chains like bracelets – content in bondage.

It is past time for us, as individuals and the Church, to release the holds that have kept us stagnant. *Well that's just how it is.*

It is imperative that we receive and maintain deliverance from anything or anyone that would hinder us from walking in the authority of Christ. Now, I know that receiving deliverance is one thing and maintaining it is something altogether different. We go to church, hear the Word and truly, truly want to do better. But when we go home, that's where the rubber meets the road. It becomes all about choices and decisions. Do we have the intestinal fortitude to break destructive habits? Should I or shouldn't I? Will I or won't I? Life is all about choices. God has set before us life and death, blessing and cursing BUT He gives us the answer. "Choose life".[1] It's an open Book test.

I am not perfect. I've made some wrong decisions and awful mistakes - been tried, tested, tempted and taunted –lived through oppressions, depressions and repossessions. But I have chosen to count every bit of it "joy".[2] Why? Because the scriptures tell me to do that and because I know God has taken every curse – every negative thing – and turned it into a blessing.[3] He did it. I <u>choose</u> to receive it.

I've taken the scenic route to arrive at some marvelous truths about what my God can not and will not do. 1. He <u>can not</u> lie. *Whatever He says <u>becomes</u> true. If it was not true before He said it, His Word makes it so.* 2. He <u>will not</u> fit into my box. *So I can take all my little 'isms' and 'schisms' somewhere and just sit on down.*

There are three reasons I chose to compile my writings. First, I am an Overcomer [4]. Secondly, the enemy desired to have me – my life, my mind and my joy. I've made it this far by the Word of God and the encouragement and support of other blood bought believers of The Christ. It's my turn to strengthen my brother.[5] My third reason for compiling my writings is for a landmark, a memorial for my children.[6] I started journaling in 1991 for them. They should not sojourn around the same mountains as I did for so long. Every round should, in fact must, go higher and higher.

Make no mistake, evil is present and bad things will continue to happen to good people. If I just hold to God's unchanging hand, He can and will continue to bring me out of every situation, but it is up to me *how* I come out. I have chosen to come out better…not bitter.

~ ~ ~

Lord I find that when I seek Your face for direction during troubled and turbulent times, You draw close to me, planting Your gifts for ministry and 'nuggets' of creativity.

"I planted the gifts and 'nuggets' before you were born.
I ordain trouble and turbulence to shift hidden treasures to the surface."

"Stir up the gifts, Lord".

"Hold on my child. It's going to be a bumpy ride".

~ ~ ~

Chapter 1: Just Who Do You Think You Are?

Silent Frustrations

While growing up at the Bethlehem Missionary Baptist Church in Graniteville, South Carolina during the '70s, I observed "church life" and the activities of those involved around me. For a long time I never put it into words but I wondered, "Is there more to "it" than this?"

Let me say right now that tradition, church activities and programs are not bad. I have a lot of wonderful memories of my childhood at Bethlehem with the youth department and Little Builders' Choir, in particular. Momma Flarrie and Mrs. Beatrice Davis took charge of the youth. And I do mean "took charge." They were mothers, overseers, caregivers, drill sergeants, psychologists, and therapists. "Hold your head up. Pull your dress down. Say your speech loud. Be quiet when grown folks is talkin'." They'd pile all of the children from the church into their two cars and take us to other youth services and activities all over town and "down the country." We were crammed in those cars very tightly, without air conditioning, I might add. Upon arrival at our destination, we'd all be hot and wrinkled but safe and sorta happy. ☺

I have particularly fond memories of our preparation for the annual Easter program. It could be likened to a mini military boot camp. They would drill us mercilessly on those speeches and songs and we'd still mess up. Somebody would forget their part, another would freeze completely but Momma Flarrie and Mrs. Bea would always say, "That's alright, baby. You did good. Ya'll give 'em hand! Stop cryin'. Let's give 'em another hand!" They taught us how to behave and how to "carry" ourselves. If they drilled and fussed hard, I have to believe that they loved us even harder.

I've always loved reading the Bible. I'm certain that I learned more in Sunday School than any other program or activity I can think of. I knew that I believed in God, that Jesus is the Son of God who died on the cross for my sins. I believed that God raised Jesus from the dead. My young mind even held to the belief that Jesus is sitting at the right hand of His Father and that He will come again for me. I could relate my understanding of the "Holy Ghost" to the churches where all the women wore long dresses and no make-up. I really thought that if I just lived right long enough, one day I would <u>become</u> holy. *Misinformed, to say the least.*

We were a church-going family. My maternal and paternal families "worked hard for the Lawd" going from church to church singin', prayin', playin' instruments and preachin'. Sundays, in particular, were full of activities – Sunday School, Morning Service, afternoon programs like choir anniversaries, Pastor appreciation services and Usher's anniversaries. The list goes on and on. I "joined the church at an early age" and began to work like everybody else around me. I sang in my home church choir and played piano for several churches over the years. I was going along as programmed but something just didn't make sense.

I was learning about Jesus, how He lived and how we should pattern ourselves after Him. Most of us went to church on Sunday and *performed* as expected but at home there were hushed conversations about "Uncle Flapjack's" girlfriend and what happened when "Aunt Jellybean" went to see Dr. Buzzard. Relatives (not play cousins) on the phone to other people talking about each other, exposing and spreading what they should have been covering with love. Adultery, jealousy, hatred and visits to the root doctor. *Hmmm.* After all the hoopin', hollerin', sweatin', spittin', stompin' and servin' the Lawd, we would return home to a defeated lifestyle. I saw and heard some things that did not make sense to me. I began to struggle with wanting to "fit in" where I was and yearning for <u>more</u>. *Am I normal?* I wanted to be more like Jesus and learn more about the Holy Ghost that I heard of, it's just this "working in the church" thing that was puzzling. The "going and doing" without change or results really didn't seem to have anything to do with the Word that I was trying to understand. So I decided, *in my finite wisdom,* that I just wouldn't worry about that. I would live my life as a good person and well, that oughta do. For a long time I just wondered and wandered.

After high school, I attended Winthrop College (Rock Hill, SC) School of Music for two years. That didn't hit the spot for me. So I joined the Air Force. Wondering and wandering. After Basic Training and Technical School, I was stationed at Myrtle Beach Air Force Base, South Carolina in 1984. One morning, I walked into the chow hall and saw the cutest, pecan tan Sergeant in the universe. "Darren" was sitting in a corner, eating a bowl of Frosted Flakes. As I walked by, I noticed a little milk rolling down the center of his chin and thought to myself – 'there is the father of my children.' We were married two years later.

The Weather Is Here, Wish You Were Beautiful

I really don't know what happened after we married. Maybe that was it – we got married. Maybe I expected too much too fast. Maybe we were both too immature. Maybe, maybe, maybe. I did not ask God to direct me. I didn't know I should do that. I thought I was supposed to meet someone, fall in love, get married, have children and stay with them so long until we started to look alike.

Whatever the case, it soon became evident that we were not on the same page. Darren was highly proficient and well respected in his career, athletic and sociable. He was very career oriented. I, on the other hand, was family focused. Our early years of marriage were full of his basketball tournaments, barbeques, friends, my nagging and begging for more attention and affection. I didn't seem to *fit in* with his lifestyle. I tried to go along with the "just hangin' out". *I wanted to be normal* The cookouts and friends were okay. I just wanted more than that. I wanted the "more" that included my husband and me working together as a team, preparing to raise a family. I was sincerely working on Cynthia but I also had my hammer and chisel in hand to help Darren out as well. *Talk about a tough nut to crack!* We were married for about two years when I had to make a decision whether or not I would reenlist. After thinking long and hard about that, I realized that in a hundred years it would not matter exactly who typed orders for military personnel but it would matter how my family had been cared for and how my children had been raised. My family's well being was the most important thing in the world to me. I decided not to reenlist.

In an effort to fill the void I thought was caused by my husband's lack of attention, I began to spend more time studying the Bible. I still wasn't thinking about working in the church at this time, nor was the thought of developing my God given gifts and talents on my mind. But I was becoming less concerned about Darren's shortcomings and more concerned about my own. In addition to my other daily Bible readings, I would always read about the virtuous woman in Proverbs 31[1] first thing in the morning and last thing at night. *That sister was baaad*   I wanted so much to be a virtuous woman and take care of my home. I thought that if I could make everything perfect enough we would live happily ever after. How empty is a Proverbs 31 woman without a Proverbs 31 man?....*Juliette without Romeo?.....J-Lo without P-Diddy...Ben...or the new guy?* ☺   I was sooo hungry   for   <u>some</u>thing...more...but what....really?

A familiar phrase for people sending postcards from their vacation at the beach is "The weather is beautiful, wish you were here." One of the Myrtle Beach radio stations turned that around as a joke for the local listeners. It was no joke for me. I was a young newlywed, with my whole life and the world ahead of me but something was still missing. I was in a seemingly beautiful place, like the man in Acts

3:1-2,[2]   right at the brink of something good…something beautiful.   But I had a problem. Why did I feel incomplete? The conditions seemed to be right. *The weather is here* What was wrong with me? *Was the gate really beautiful or was it just called that?*

Crossing Over

In 1989, we were stationed at Kadena Air Base, Okinawa, Japan. When we got the orders, I remember thinking that we would be going to a primitive place. Our first few days there were quite a culture shock for me. Until that time, I had never spent any substantial amount of time outside South Carolina. When the taxi driver picked us up at the airport, I noticed he had something like turret's syndrome. Every few seconds his eyes would blink and his entire body would jerk really hard. It was scary enough when we were loading the luggage into the car. It got real scary as we zipped through traffic. Add to his blinking and twitching, the fact that Okinawans drive on the opposite side of the road than we do in the U.S.! I remember calling home to let everyone know that we had arrived safely – no thanks to our convulsing cab driver. The most dangerous leg of the journey to our new home was <u>not</u> the twenty hour flight across the Pacific. It was the fifteen minute cab ride to the hotel. I was exhausted! I yelled in the phone, "These people drive on the wrong side of the road!"

It didn't take long to realize that we needed to get some transportation and I needed to be able to get around and do what was necessary to set up the household while Darren was working. I took the driver's course offered on base and got my international driver's license within a few weeks. During my next call home, I proudly announced, "I'm zipping around like a native."

During that time of settling in and getting used to the traffic, I was also looking for a Church to attend. In addition to all of the available base chapel services for every denomination, there were several non-denominational Churches thriving on the island. A friend invited us to visit Word of God Christian Center. *Oh...my...goodness* I had never heard the Word of God dissected and taught with such simplicity and power. Pastor Paul Terry was a no muss, no fuss kind of preacha. He and his wife Kathy had been led by God to make their home in Okinawa and they lived on the economy with their five children. I found the Terrys to be powerful people of faith and wisdom. It was under the teaching of this ministry that I first experienced the power of praise and worship. As the praise team led the congregation to usher in the Holy Spirit, people would receive deliverance and healing right in their seats. No one touched them. *Hmmm.* One Sunday, just as Pastor Terry stood to minister, a lady in the congregation began to scream. I really didn't know what was going on. I assumed she was just caught up in the Spirit. *It was a spirit, alright.* What was interesting, was how Pastor Terry handled it. He did not get flustered. I don't remember his exact words but in a calm, firm voice he commanded the spirit to be quiet and leave. No screaming. No hollering. No spit. I don't know if he even looked at her. He simply exercised his authority through the blood of Jesus the Christ and that spirit had to obey.

Now that's what I'm talkin' 'bout – Power!

Pastor Terry taught powerfully about the gifts and fruits of the Holy Spirit, the power of the tongue (what you say), forgiveness, the blood of Jesus, spiritual warfare and strongholds. What I like most was how he used practical application to demonstrate the Word. To make it clear that God is not, concerned about outward appearance, he once preached in a T-Shirt, cut-off denim shorts, and tennis shoes. I almost fell out of my chair. We made it through service that day without him being struck by lightning so I thought it might be okay. *He'd better not try that where I came from* I'd been in church all my life and honestly, I'd never heard tell of <u>this</u> stuff he was talkin'. I clearly remember praying and asking God to show me if this "Word" was okay.

The Spirit of the Lord reminded me of my self-righteousness when I screamed "these people drive on the wrong side of the road." *How dare they not fit into my box!* It suddenly occurred to me that if I were to go driving down Gate Two Street on the side of the road I thought was correct, I would be the cause of major destruction. *Who said they were wrong?* It just wasn't the side I was accustomed to. I believe God took me from the States, family, friends, and everything that was familiar and comfortable to let me know that there was much more in the world than I had seen. It took that experience to help me realize that there is much more to God, too, than I had experienced to that point in my life. Everything familiar was gone. I had to take a fresh new look at a lot of things – especially me. I was holding on to things that I really needed to let go of like opinions, unforgiveness, old hurts and habits. Some things I didn't even realize were there until the light of God's Word hit me in the face.

The Word of God was tearing down strongholds in my life. For instance, I had never even talked about, let alone dealt with, being molested as a child. Nor had I acknowledged within myself the pain and effects of my parents' divorce after seventeen years of marriage. During a lot of my young years I seem to have been "halt between two opinions", if you will. On the one hand, I remember being basically ignored by some I wanted so desperately to include me. *I didn't fit in there* On the other hand, oftentimes where I was included I'd observe some patterns and lifestyle that didn't "line-up" even with my young spirit. Because I was a child and raised to "stay in my place" I thought something must be wrong with me. *So I wasn't normal* As an adult, I was trying to cope with all these symptoms but I had never looked at their cause. It is so true that light and darkness have no fellowship. The more I sought God, the more "stuff" came to the surface. Apparently, I did not really know either person standing at the altar on that extremely hot July day in 1986 – *should've been a sign* So then three years later, as I began to shed layers of "stuff", I found myself living in a strange place with not one but two strange people – a husband and ME.

Darren and I did manage to have two beautiful and brilliant children while in Okinawa. We just never connected as husband and wife. How could we? We did not share the same vision for life and family.[3] For one thing, we had different viewpoints of the atmosphere that should have been set in our home. I wanted nothing more than to be an at-home mommy while the children were young. My dream was to have them grow up with memories of smelling fresh breads, hearing a lot of laughter and feeling secure. Darren felt that if I worked, we could have <u>more.</u> I wanted more, too. In fact, my intent has always been to have it <u>all</u>. I just wasn't trying to have it <u>all</u> at the same time. If you stuff too many different foods in your mouth at once, you can't really taste and enjoy any of it. I wanted to mold the home and children while I still had the opportunity to influence them then go out and conquer the rest of the world. ☺ I had this really clear picture in my mind of what our home should look, feel and even smell like. *Too bad I didn't marry a mind reader.*

I used to have a recurring dream in which Darren would be standing in front of me smiling very calmly. I would kick, scratch, bite and fight him with all of my strength – so much so, that I would sometimes sit up in bed panting and gasping for air. I had this dream one or two times in the years prior to moving to Okinawa. But once we were there and I was being filled with the Word, that dream came more frequently and with more intensity. That went on for many months until Pastor Terry taught a series on Ephesians 6:12[4] Voila! My problem was not with Darren and no matter how "right" I *thought* I was about wanting him to align himself with the Word and stand as the priest of our home, it was not mine to do. So I finally stopped trying to nag him into the

Kingdom but I still had a lot of growing to do. I needed some clarity and direction about things in my own life.

Sitting under the anointed ministry of Pastor Terry was either the best or worst thing that could have happened to me. I always refer to my exposure to that ministry as the beginning of the end. It was the beginning to the end of my wondering and wandering. If I had not received that mind transforming Word, maybe I could have eventually stopped yearning and been able to adjust to programmed church life. But there was no turning back now. Not only was I convinced that there really was more, I was determined to attain it. I began to recognize some strongholds in my life caused by family and generational curses – divorce, living in lack, low esteem, infidelity – that were affecting me and declared, "I WILL NOT PASS THIS JUNK ON TO MY CHILDREN"! I sought to be filled with the Holy Spirit, I needed to plug into THE power source. I needed it and wanted it. *Something* was going on the spirit realm and, like it or not, I was a part of it. I had to be equipped and prepared. I began to fast, pray and practice my praise. Every morning, I envisioned the devil dropping his head and letting out a loud, excruciating scream, "Oh nooooo, not *her* again!" The warfare had begun and I was in for the fight of my life. Little did I know that I would have to one day fight <u>for</u> my life.

One night I was heavily burdened with *something*. I cried, moaned and lay before God all night. I needed some answers and was prepared to wrestle. God won. He always does. This marked the spot where I answered. I recall uttering something like, "If I gotta do *this*, I want to be affective. Please God, show me." I knew that there were enough people singing just to be singing – enough people preaching just because they could talk and carry a "tune". I was not sure at all what, exactly, I was to do. But I knew that I had to do *it*. If I didn't, nothing else would ever make sense. Some time during the night it was as if a warm, fluffy blanket covered me. I don't remember hearing anything audible but I *heard* with every fiber of my being, **"There are no shortcuts. There is no compromise."** That Word did not encompass me. It consumed me. The Voice was not in the room. It was in me.

No shortcuts, no compromise. All the way in or all the way out. *Either we is or we ain't.* No shortcuts, no compromise. I was between The Rock and a hard place. It wasn't a matter of me having the Word. The Word had me and the gifts that I had tried to forget or deny were being stirred. *Hmmm.* Is it possible to stir a pot without disturbing its contents? *I don't think so.*

Just Who Do You Think You Are?

By the time we moved to England in '92, I had grown enough in the Word to know that God hates divorce and the saved spouse could very well win the unsaved spouse by their lifestyle. We had not cultivated the warm, happy home I had always envisioned, but I was making a sincere effort to be the Christian wife and mother that I should. In my mind, it wasn't about Darren or me. It was about the Word of God and my children. *Darren was just gonna have to be happy, whether he liked it or not.* ☺ I knew it would be good for me to use my pent up energy and frustrations constructively so I considered going back to school. I wanted to be ready to re-enter the workforce when the children started school. Every time we talked about it, there would be some hindrance. Money – I wasn't working. Who would care for the children? It just never seemed to work out. We continued to grow further and further apart. I took care of the house and children all day. As soon as I'd see Darren's car lights in the driveway, I'd take about three or four Excedrin P.M. and go to sleep. That was my escape and the routine for many weeks.

After about a year in England, Darren made arrangements for the children and me to return to South Carolina. Before our departure, I learned that he had been having an affair with a female co-worker. Even though we were already in the process of separating, I was devastated. I had never shook and cried like that before in my life. To make things worse, he and this co-worker were supposedly riding to their lunch time class together everyday while I was at home cooking and cleanTing. *I spelt it just like I would have said it! Hmpf, hmpf, hmpf. (You gotta shake your head from side to side, too.)*

For a long time I was like Eve before she was...well...herself. Notice Genesis 2:21-3:7.[5] Eve was a rib, a woman and a wife before she made one simple, yet catastrophic decision that affects all of humankind. THEN she got a name.[6] Like Eve, I had made a major decision before I had a real identity of my own. I was somebody's daughter, wife and mother without even a clue as to who or whose I was. *If your eagle egg is somehow dropped into the middle of a chicken farm, hatched and raised there, that does not make you a chicken. That makes you an out of place eagle.* So, just who do you think <u>you</u> are?

Divorce was not a reality for me at this point. I <u>couldn't</u> be divorced. I was a Christian woman – faithful to my husband, with a sincere desire to be an instrument fit for use by the Master. I had already told the devil, in no uncertain terms, that he was not going to destroy my family and continue the vicious cycle. Divorce was simply not an option. I didn't think about what was going to happen beyond this pending separation. Maybe I wasn't thinking at all beyond my present pain. No plan. No nothing. Just...nothing.

During one of our last conversations, Darren told me that he just didn't want "it". Ten years and two babies later - - you just don't want it. Well good morning Leah![7] It's been a long night. Right, wrong, good, bad, indifferent, beautiful or ugly, you gave Jacob all that you had – You. He just didn't want it. I know you gave your best...everything. It wasn't enough. Maybe you should have asked – I mean, before you gave so completely – "Will you still love me tomorrow?" You were acceptable when masked in darkness. The Light is shining on you now. What ya' gonna do? Change your hair color? Try a new perfume? You can not stop the breaking of day. If you could remain in yesterday or last night – even that might be alright. But it's tomorrow. *Hmmm. All of us ain't "Rachels". We don't come with a beautiful face or pretty story. But there's something...*

What could I do? I didn't hate Darren. *Maybe a little for a minute...okay, okay maybe a lot for a long time. But I don't now. Really* ☺ Like Leah, I gave all I had – Me, to someone who, through no real fault of his own, did not – would not – could not <u>see</u> me. Neither of us knew what we were getting with the other. I didn't know that he was not capable of providing what I <u>really</u> needed – no man can. He didn't know that he married a mighty woman of God, called to wreak havoc on Satan's kingdom.

Three women, whose beginnings (their former) were clouded in doubt, bad decisions, rejection, guilt and shame. Eve's latter birthed life.[8] Leah's latter birthed Judah (Praise)[9] and ultimately, The Christ.[10] I, too, have something inside me that must be birth into reality. *Hmmm.*[11]

"Life" happened to me and I was left with a broken heart, shattered dreams and one simple decision to make. Lay down and die or get up and fight?

Chapter 2: There's No Place Like Home

Computer generated drawing by Darius Mitchell

There's No Place Like Home

The flight home to South Carolina did not even seem real. I cried most of the way. I stepped off that plane with two small children and a ton of emotional baggage. My instincts kicked in. I hit the ground running. Determined to allow my frustrations to catapult me into success, I got busy. I had a vision, ideas, energy and wanted to surround myself with positive and supportive people. Although hurting, I had enough enthusiasm to share a few ideas about ministry and business with some family and close friends. Wrong move! I was hit with a barrage of fire--you're too young, too old, under educated, over educated. You can't do that, you're divorced with two small children and no money. Business - - ministry? Hah! And PUHLEESE don't let me say anything about my desire to remarry. "You already got a husband. Ain't nobody gonna want you anyway with two children. No man wants the responsibility of raising somebody else's children." I didn't clean up right, I didn't take care of the kids properly. I was treated as a failure.

As Christians, we are admonished to "resist the devil". The problem is too many of us have an unrealistic image of Satan, your adversary, the devil. When's the last time you saw a little man running around in a red suit with horns and a pitchfork? He is <u>not</u> easily recognized. He <u>is</u> white, black, Asian, rich and poor. He does not restrict his activities to any particular place or group of people. He's subtle and will quietly, but most assuredly set up shop in our homes, schools, places of work and even worship. Little by little, capitalizing on every opportune moment since the day you were born. He set the wheels in motion <u>before</u> you were born. Too many of us have been held captive by patterns that did not begin with us. That's sad but the real tragedy is that we continue the destructive cycles because we don't recognize them or we simply refuse to do what is necessary to break them. Instead, we reinforce the strongholds with wrong thinking and disobedience. A little here. A little there.

I recognized some of the strongholds and curses while living away, the spirits of jealousy and bondage. Now, I was right back in the middle of it all. I had hit the ground running. Now I was just on the ground...depressed! The enemy had me rocking and reeling for awhile. A long while. I didn't get the emotional or spiritual support I expected. *Nobody can give you what they don't have.* I wanted so badly to be connected - to feel cared for and protected. I longed to be planted in a ministry – a safe place - to settle down and birth all the things that were inside of me so that I could grow. I had sooo much growing to do.

Well, a part of growing up is experiencing aches and pains. One pain, in particular, I had to experience was being hurt by church people. I've often heard, "Love thy neighbor as thyself". I've come to realize that I don't want some people to love me the way they love themselves. Far too many Christians, men and women, suffer with low self esteem and lack of self love. There are a lot of hurting and confused Christians, in the pulpit and the pew and hurting people can only do what they know - hurt other people. So then here I come with a sack full of my own hurts, looking for the opportunity to share my newly discovered, however small, buds of ministry. I was not prepared for the reception. "Hmpf, with them two chirren and no husband, *call herself* working in the church leading praise and worship." *That's the thing, I didn't call myself. I've been hurt and I'm trying to praise my way out of this!* I was broken and seeking refuge among the saints. What I often found was criticism and more rejection. I remember talking with a person one day who was letting me know "in their way" that they did not approve of my "standing up in front of the church" being divorced. I stood my ground in front of them (*I cried later*) and simply said, "Okay, either the blood of Jesus cleanses or it doesn't." My life had fallen apart and I was not in a position to dilly dally. I was trying to be a good soldier in the army of the Lord, and by far, my worst hurts and most devastating blows came from my family and fellow soldiers - church folks.

While in Okinawa, the Word made more sense to me....for me. Now I was back to wondering and wandering. I know one reason for my inability to settle into a ministry stemmed from personal issues of rejection and hurt. I am just as certain though that somewhere along the way I learned to be careful who I allow to *feed* me. I have attended more than a few churches trying to fit in -Baptist, Methodist, Pentecostal, Apostolic Overcoming Holy. *Oh Lord, why can't I just be normal – fit in with somebody?* I have been called a church hopper *and probably much worse.* I remember trying to "hang in there" at a particular ministry partly because it was where I wanted to be and partly because I was concerned about what people would say about me for leaving. I respected the Pastor, my children were involved and it seemed to be a good place to settle in and serve. The only problem was that I wasn't supposed to be there. Church is not a social club. *Oh Lord, that my desire would become lost in Your will, is my prayer.*

I have likened some of my ministry experiences to spiritual prostitution. Some pastors were more concerned with building their kingdom rather than The Kingdom. The logic, as explained to me was, "you gotta have a 'draw' and everybody loves good singing." When did the church start believing in gimmicks? *And I, if I be lifted up from the earth will draw all men unto me.*[1] *That's your "draw".* I was concerned that some leadership demonstrated little regard for the condition of the precious souls in their care and no concern at all for the attitudes and spirits of those leading the congregation into worship. They just want you to sound good, get the people worked up. My "job" was to make sure the choir sound was good and oh yeah, "the color for Sunday is red." There is nothing wrong with improving the sound, look and presentation of a music ministry, as long as it does not come at the expense of compromise. *There is no compromise.* For too long, the popular opinion has been as long as we look good, all is well. But effective ministry can not stand on frills, bells and whistles. It's like putting on perfume without taking a bath - trying to cover what will eventually show up anyway. I was only important some places as long as I produced what was wanted and would be paid for my services when "man" was satisfied. *Hmmm.* What if this is more than a job to me? What if God has called me to something that doesn't include pleasing you? What if I'm trying to grow up – toward the Son? *Some people don't mind you growing as long as you don't outgrow your usefulness to them.*

Know this. You can't just go plopping your spiritual babies (seeds for ministry from God) down any ole where. When I gave birth to my children, I sought counsel from qualified "baby delivering" doctors. I committed my medical care and that of my unborn children to them. They were trained for just that sort of thing. I trusted their judgement and followed their directions even when I did not want to. Dr. "J"

(Julius Erving), although highly proficient as a professional basketball player, is not the doctor I would have chosen to deliver my babies. Carl Malone (the Mailman) delivers – but not babies. I would not have entrusted my medical well being to him either. It really does not mean that one pastor or church is more spiritual or better than another. If one church had everything that everybody needed, we'd all be sittin' in the same church. *Right, Brother Stokes?* Put on your spiritual ears and hear me when I say, "If the Spirit of the Lord tells you to get up and get thee going, you'd better hop like a Mexican jumping bean."

While nursing the pain inflicted by church people, I had to learn how to love and respond to the needs of those same people. No matter how bad they talked about me. Jesus walked among people who mistreated and mishandled Him. Self-righteous religious leaders and skeptical church folks. *Hmmm* There was also a worshipping prostitute and a repentant thief. The "everybodies" and the "nobodies". "Everybody" wanna go to heaven but "nobody" wants to die. "Everybody" wants to reign with Christ but "nobody" wants to be crucified. News flash – to be affective in the ministry of the Gospel of Jesus Christ, you <u>must</u> die[2] and if you spend any amount of time around church folk, you *will* be crucified. Since God orders the steps of the righteous, I have to believe that I needed to experience all of it before any of it could make sense. *No shortcuts. No compromise.*

Why are church folk so mean though? Why did Saul hate David? Saul was king. David was a shepherd. It wasn't anything physical or material that caused Saul's jealousy and hatred of David. It had less to do with David and more to do with Saul. Saul's disobedience and rejection of God caused him to lose his relationship with the prophet Samuel, his position as king[3] and his mind.[4] I would venture to say, most of the hate that tends to exude from fellow Christians is not intentional. It is borne out of their pain, confusion and inability (for whatever reason) to receive the liberties provided by Christ. Example, most of us have been conditioned to stay in the box. Don't rock the boat. Wait on the Lord. Jesus is saying, *"What is a box?" "Who needs a boat?" "I'm waiting on you."* These poor people are trying so hard to stay where some misguided soul (someone highly respected like a pastor, teacher or parent) put them, but the Spirit of the Lord is calling them out. They are torn – in pain. So, they wonder and wander, bumping into things causing more damage to themselves and others. When a "wonderer" happens to make the acquaintance of someone who is not normal, according to their standards, they'd rather kill them than help achieve anything for the Kingdom. *Who said they're driving on the wrong side of the road?*

Now, the biggest problem with all of this is that the "wonderer" and the "abnormal" person are not strangers to each other. They go to school together, go to church and out to eat together. Sometimes they live together. During the Gulf War, the term "friendly fire" became popular. *I don't care how friendly the fire, pain is pain and the target is just as dead.* Saul calls for David to come play the harp then throws a spear at him

before he can get to the vamp.[5]   One day
they're ringing your phone off the hook to
come work with their music ministry for the
choir anniversary, the next day they're
scandalizing your name. David said it best in
Psalm 55:12-14[6] (paraphrased): *"Oh Lawd! My
friend hurt me – hurt me bad. It wasn't an enemy.
I could have understood that better. At least I could
have avoided an enemy and not exposed my inner
most feelings and dreams....Nooooo, this was
someone who knew me well and I thought I knew
them. We go to the same church. They hurt me - -
hurt me bad."*

Somewhere during all the madness, the divorce
from Darren became final. I was functioning,
going to work, meetings, choir rehearsals,
taking the kids to dance, music lessons and
parties but sinking deeper and deeper into

depression. I was tired and thought I wanted to die. I seriously contemplated suicide. One night, I decided that I would take a whole lot of sleeping pills *(If I can just hold out 'till tomorrow)* then run a bathtub full of water, *(If I can just keep the faith through the night)* get in and just go. *(If I can just hold out 'till tomorrow)* I lay on the sofa and cried and cried. *(Everything will be, be alright)* Another loooong night. At some point though, I realized that my children were going to get up the next morning, come into my room (as usual) and they would find me. That's the <u>only</u> thing that stopped me. I couldn't do that to my children. So I continued to "function."

In a women's meeting one night, some ladies where expressing frustration because their husbands were not supportive of their church work. They talked about arguments and discord in their households. One lady talked about a time when arguments with her husband would become physical. One of the sisters said, "Well, he is just going to have to understand that I have to do what the Lord says do." So I asked the question, "Who says that everything we do, the Lord said do?" Mostly they all just looked at me. I don't think I ever did get an answer. I was not trying to be smart or funny at all. I really wanted to know how to be sure that I was in line with the will of God. I had been trained – conditioned to go, go, go and do, do, do. The more committees you serve on, the more "saved" you are. *Right?* I found myself at a point where I wanted – needed to just be. It can be so hard to break the cycle of old habits and patterns. As the twig is bent, so grows the tree.

Who's Ya' Daddy?

My life was already in a tizzy. Then, after a rather brief but traumatic illness, my Daddy died. If you ever need to see a living description of a "daddy's girl" that would be me. Although my parents divorced after seventeen years of marriage, they remarried after being divorced for nine years. Daddy was not a saint by any stretch of the imagination. If I tried to tell some of the stories, that would be another book. He had his share of vices and ills but he loved me and "Papa's best helpers" (my children). He didn't mind letting us – or anyone else for that matter – know it.

On October 2, 1996, family, friends and on-lookers gathered at the house. Daddy held clear and articulate conversation until his last breath. After saying goodbye to all of us, he said that he just wanted to rest. *Oh, that I had wings like a dove.* I was laying on the pillow with him. I watched his eyes roll. His tongue thickened and the color of his fingernails changed to a darkest blue. His hands began to cool then – what I had heard my grandma 'nem talk about – the death rattle, a slight gurgling. If death can be beautiful, his was.

When life returned to normal – whatever that is. I could see God's hand at work. It was necessary that the kids and I had the few short years back home before Daddy died. It was necessary for me to have the opportunity to drive back and forth to Charleston with him for tests and surgery. *Sometimes we talked. Sometimes we talked. Other times we were just quiet* I had to be available to go with him for chemotherapy and radiation. It was good for me to see my Daddy go from taking care of everybody to being taken care of. After many years of watching him help people with so many things and traveling to sing and preach, I needed to witness the pain and rejection he experienced by people he thought were his closest friends. In his last painful days and even hours, I had to hear my Daddy quoting scripture and singing hymns. One of the most difficult experiences in my life was the catalyst for tremendous spiritual growth. Daddy's death caused me to make some assessments in my own life. I was forced to look at people, life and death differently.

In my humble opinion, one colossal mistake we make in families is that we don't talk about the real stuff. We talk about events, happenings and other people but can not bring ourselves to confront and deal with things that are killing us and our children. We take that same mentality to church. We have anniversaries, meetings and services without getting to the meat of the matter. *I already said ain't nothing wrong with church programs and activities.* I'm just saying that, we seem to have settled into the mindset that it's easier to <u>have</u> church than to <u>be</u> the church.

It wasn't until the last few months of Daddy's life that I began to get a glimpse of the pain, physical and emotional, that he suffered as a child. I could sometimes still see that pain in my Daddy's eyes as he continued to look for acceptance and approval from some of <u>his</u> family. He stood in the yard one day waiting and waiting for one of them who had promised to take him to a doctor's appointment. I guess he didn't <u>fit in</u> their schedule that day. *No one can give you what they don't have.*

"In the year King Uzziah died, I saw also the Lord..."[7] I remember hearing Rev. Doug Slaughter preach this message soon after losing Daddy. He made it *live.* The experience of Daddy's death caused me to set some landmarks in my life. This marked the spot where I knew God was calling me to spread my wings and launch into deeper waters but I was afraid. *Launch out into the deep? I can't even swim. Anyway, it's all I can do to "keep it where I got it" and You want me to do what? People talk about me, misjudge my motives. I don't have the resources and I'm just not ready.* **I didn't ask you to swim. I'm the One <u>keeping you</u>. People talked about and misjudged Me. I AM THE Source.** I was like the dog that had been chained to a tree for a very long time. When he was finally released, he still would not venture away from the tree because he had been conditioned to stay there. In the year my King Uzziah died, I embraced my release from tradition, gossip and trying to fit in. Read my lips and hear me when I scream – GET AWAY FROM THAT TREE! God is calling you to higher heights and deeper depths in Him.

I still had to do a lot of soul searching. So many things had happened in my life that I could not control. Some things, on the other hand, I had allowed to happen. No need worrying about that now. I decided, from this point forward, I am not responsible for other people's actions, not every toward me, but I am completely responsible for how I allow their actions to affect me. I learned how not to receive some things.

My family, Daddy in particular, had been well known in our area for singing the gospel. There are still some people who genuinely love me simply because I am his daughter, while others genuinely do not like me for the same reason. I am often asked, "Do you sing like your Daddy?" Or I'll hear one person tell another, "You know whose child that is? She's just like her Daddy." *Hmmm....* What did *that* mean? What does it matter? The important thing is who really is my <u>DADDY</u>? Am I growing more and more like Him?

Why did Jesus ask His disciples, "Who do men say that I am?"[8] Surely it was not to validate Himself. That question led to a divine revelation through Peter. The opinion of people does not matter. Did the "certain woman" care what it looked like when she knelt in a house full of people who were whispering about her as she worshipped the Christ?[9] She focused on her purpose. Nobody could talk her up, down or out. You go girl. Handle yo' binness. *You know I spelt it like I would have said it.* Anyway, I stopped receiving other people's opinion of me – good or bad.

With all of that in mind, I set my focus on trying to find out, specifically, what God had for me to do. In the midst of making this mental and lifestyle change, I heard Bishop T.D. Jakes say in a message, "sometimes we get so busy with the work of the Lord until we forget about the Lord of the work." *Hallelujah!* I had gotten so busy until I was missing out on a lot of my intimate time with God. That's where the power is and it was quietly slipping away in all the hoopla.

Upon returning home, I had fallen back into rush here. Run there. I had to <u>decide</u> that the years of struggling to fit in and be normal were done. It's impossible to measure up to everybody's expectations anyway– they keep changing. When Jesus died on the cross He said, "It is finished." Had <u>all</u> the people of His time been healed – saved or even fed? No. But He had completed what <u>He</u> was sent to do. I prayed, *"Lord please, establish my goings."* I *want to be like my DADDY.*

If my goal is to become more like Christ, then it stands to reason that I would <u>be</u> more like Christ - rejected by people in general, by family in particular *He did not fit in.* Remember how

Jesus came to his own people and they did not receive Him?[10] They wondered and speculated about who He was. Was He qualified to forgive sins? *Yip yap. Yip yap.* One day the people were shouting Hosanna in the streets. Next they were screaming "crucify Him!" Crucified by the very ones He was sent to minister to and buried in a dark, cold place by well meaning friends. *Hmpf, just like my DADDY.*

During the long years of church hoppin' and soul searching, "life" had once again brought some unforeseen and unfortunate circumstances. I was tired and felt so alone. The one person on this earth who I thought could and knew would be there for me, was dead. I was left with a broken heart, shattered dreams and one simple decision to make. Lay down and die or get up and fight?

Chapter 3: When A Lie Becomes The Truth

"Who changed the truth of God into a lie…"?
Romans 1:24a

Perilous Times

So, I returned home and found myself surrounded by attitudes, and behaviors that I had learned were not healthy or productive. In addition to that, I realized that it was much easier to say I had forgiven some past issues while living an ocean away from those "issues". It was an entirely different challenge learning to love what I didn't like. *Yes Lord, "forgiveness" is more than a notion.*

I tried to close my eyes and ears to a lot of things. I just kept thinking that I would get on my feet and move away. Far away. That would be my escape. *Yeah right, Jonah.* Every time I tried, something would happen and I would find myself right back where I started. *Hmm, a cycle. Why can't I just get away from all this nonsense and live a quiet, peaceful life? I*

didn't call you to run from anything. I sought God to provide a way of escape for <u>my</u> comfort. *Why am I stuck?* My attention was being drawn to *other* things in the scriptures. **You are planted.** I tried to close my eyes to that as well. But several passages got stuck in my craw and just wouldn't move.

2 Timothy 3:1-6

But mark this: There will be terrible times in the last days. People will be lovers of themselves, lovers of money, boastful, proud, abusive, disobedient to their parents, ungrateful, unholy, without love, unforgiving, slanderous, without self-control, brutal, not lovers of the good, treacherous, rash, conceited, lovers of pleasure rather than lovers of God – having a form of godliness, but denying its power. Have nothing to do with them. They are the kind who worm their way into homes and gain control over weak- willed women, who are loaded down with sins and are swayed by all kinds of evil desires.

The Word is everywhere – as plain as the nose on your face. We gasp with disgust at the headlines – 'Mother kills baby' or 'Teen kills parents'. There's so much more going on than the things that scream for our attention. Subtle things that creep into our houses and hearts, causing us to live outside of God's will and beneath our privilege. *We protest abortion clinics but continue to gossip and kill fellow believers with our tongue.* Most of these "things" have slipped in, unnoticed. When did we become lovers of own selves and proud, *It's my prerogative...what's in it for me?* Incontinent, *No need for restraint. If it feels good, do it with whomever... whenever* Truce(peace)breakers *Do you know anybody who just stays on the phone keeping up mess? Maybe there's someone in your office who's not happy unless there's some drama going on* Can we not see what's going on? *Wake up Sampson. They're messin' with your strength – your power.*[1] We are being lulled into a powerless position when there's a conspiracy -- all out war going on! Don't be offended. I'm not pointing fingers. I said <u>we</u>. Will we ever move from continuously asking God to <u>work on</u> us to allowing Him to <u>work through</u> us? Why do we keep waiting on the Lord to do what He gave <u>us</u> the power and authority to do?

Jesus left His home in glory, took on human form. He walked among men, teaching, preaching and performing wondrous works. He was crucified, died and buried in a borrowed tomb. Jesus conquered death, hell and the grave. He stopped back by earth, to let his disciples know everything was cool – just like He said it would be.[2] He then ascended to heaven to resume His ordained position at the right hand of His Father where He is now – right now, interceding on our behalf. He didn't leave us high and dry though, He sent the Comforter, His Spirit, to keep us informed on everything that He and the Father discuss so that we'll be able to make sound daily decisions. *Whew! He's done all that. The least I can do is stop* _____ *(You fill in the blank).*

The believers' stand in these last days is crucial. No shortcuts. No compromise.

Ezekiel 3:17-19
"Son of man, I have made you a watchman for the house of Israel; so hear the word I speak and give them warning from me. When I say to a wicked man, 'You will surely die,' and you do not warn him or speak out to dissuade him from his evil ways in order to save his life, that wicked man will die for his sin, and I will hold you accountable for his blood. But if you do warn the wicked man and he does not

turn from his wickedness or from his evil ways, he will die for his sin; but you will have saved yourself.

Ezekiel 3:17-19 reminds me of the nursery rhyme Little Boy Blue.

> Little Boy Blue
> Come blow your horn.
> The sheep's in the meadow.
> The cow's in the corn.
> Where's the little boy who looks after the sheep?
> Under the haystack, fast asleep.
> Will you wake him?
> No, not I.
> If I do, he sure will cry.

This little boy, a keeper of sheep, is sleeping on the job. The sheep are out of place. Cows have no business in the corn. Will you wake him – let him know what's going on? No, I don't want to get involved. I see the destruction and devastation but it's not my place to say anything. Let somebody else do it. How long do you think we should wait before waking him? It's looking pretty bad already.

Revelation 22:10-11
Then he told me, "Do not seal up the words of the prophecy of this book, because the time is near. Let him who does wrong continue to do wrong; let him who is vile continue to be vile; let him who does right continue to do right; and let him who is holy continue to be holy."

The Watchmen are asleep and the church – the sheep – are running amuck. We're fast approaching the time when it won't even matter anymore. If you're righteous, stay righteous. If you're holy, stay holy. If you're filthy, well just stay right there. Keep on doing whatever it is you're doing. *"And, Behold, I come quickly..."* [3]

Warfare of the Spirits
What is it that has the Watchmen distracted?

Why is it we cannot stay awake long enough to give the warning? Could it be that we, the believers, do not actually believe that spiritual warfare is real?

Exactly what is spiritual warfare? Let's start with what it is <u>not</u>.

Spiritual warfare is not mystical or magical. Neither is it physical. Natural abilities will be of no use in this fight. We should not attempt to engage in spiritual warfare armed with a list of achievements, committee affiliations or good deeds. Simply going to church every Sunday learning program and protocol will not do anything to prepare us for spiritual warfare. Learning procedure while growing up in church is far removed from the process of the Church growing in you. Once committed to being a follower of Christ, it is vital – essential – imperative that you begin to fill your mind with the things of Christ. Why? Because you are a new creature. The way you used to act, think and live does not apply anymore.[4] You no longer fight on the street. You now fight with mighty weapons in the heavenlies.[5] Spiritual warfare is, indeed, spiritual.

I have been overwhelmed thinking about spiritual warfare but I now know the Holy Spirit will lead and guide you into <u>all</u> truth. I would like to share three things that help me during my battles.

1. Keep your relationship with Christ   pure. I believe that the key to any successful relationship is communication. Have a little talk with Jesus everyday. Several times a day

is alright. When you mess up say, "Lord, I messed up. Please show me how to do better." Real communication works both ways. *You can't do all the talking.* Listen for His reply.[6]

2. Learn whose you are then exercise the authority given to you in His name.[7]

3. Study the Blood covenant of Christ and how it applies to believers. The power is in the Blood. Learn the value of the Blood.[8 and 9]

Follow through on the three things I just mentioned requires effort. We can not only hear the Word while in church, we <u>must</u> hold on to it once we get home and apply it to our daily situations – lifestyle. Read the Word, study the Word, pray the Word, sing the Word - - *aw shucks, go ahead – yodel the Word.* Filling your atmosphere and mind with the Word of God will strengthen your spirit man for the spiritual battles that are sure to come.

Your spirit is somewhat like your physical body in that food (substance) is required for proper functioning. If you feed your physical body junk, it will eventually show the effects. Likewise, your spirit man will show the effects of what's being deposited there. The health and fitness of your spirit will determine how well you are able to stand in spiritual warfare. Why is a healthy spirit important? Because that is where decisions like 'will I lift my hands in praise or won't I' are made. 'Will I humble and submit all of me to the Holy Spirit' is determined in your spirit. Intellect could reason an answer one way or the other. Your spirit will respond based on how you've been conditioned to think. So, what's going on in your mind?

> "Since the mind holds the secrets of soaring, the enemy of our soul has made the human mind the bulls-eye of his target. By affecting the way we think, he is able to keep our lives on a mediocre level."
> Charles Swindoll, Living Above the Level of Mediocrity

A healthy mind is the key to a healthy spirit. The messages you've heard all your life through people and or media affect the way you think – good or bad. The messages don't always have to be audible. Stereotypes and even attitudes of indifference have a way of shaping our thought processes and productivity. If I perceive that you do not expect much of me, chances are I will stop striving at the "not much" mark. In the same way, if I can get you comfortable in bondage, happy to stay there even when you've been made free. "After all the mess you've been in, you really think that a perfect God could love you?" "Did you see how she just looked at you? She's talking about you." *But she's crossed-eyed and didn't even see you. Wrong thinking.* Once the enemy has you in his camp – caught up in a cycle of wrong thinking, he's got you. He does not make you do anything. It was likely the enemy's influence behind the wrong messages that were fed into your mind then settled in your spirit, but you, consciously or subconsciously, decided to buy it. You thought wrong, then acted wrong. *You didn't have to slap her* Still, accepting the enemy's lies is not spiritual warfare. *If you're doing what I want you to do, there's no need for us to fight.* The warfare begins when you decide to leave the enemy's camp.

Okay, what is spiritual warfare? It is the pulling of your spirit, with the strength of the Holy Spirit as your anchor, away from the evil nature and tendencies of Satan's spirit. It is, ultimately, a holy battle between the God of good and the forces of evil to "occupy" your spirit. The battleground? Your mind. Guard it well.[10]

Lame Of His Feet

One of my most sincere desires is to be covered in a marital relationship. To be married and nurture a healthy, happy family is the one thing I've always wanted. It's not the only thing I've ever wanted. But is the one thing I've always wanted. The "wife" part of me is still there and longing for fulfillment. I am convinced that God will not only bless me with that desire of my heart, but He will allow me to be a blessing and very suitable companion to my husband as well.

Several years ago, I took a sheet of paper and drew a line down the middle. On one side, I made a list of my character traits, gifts and talents. On the other side, I listed desired traits for my mate. With that, and given the fact that I positively loathe "busy work" - being with someone just to say, "I got a man", I used my God-given organizational skills to develop a handy little "man categorization system". *I imagine God gets a real belly laugh when I help Him out.*

Category 1:
The "good catch but not the right one" man. He's nice but now that I've learned more about who I am in Christ, that just won't work. Been

there. Done that. Got the T-shirt and DVD.

Category 2:

The "I'm going through my second childhood and just wanna play around" man. Not happening. You're too old for that and I'm too good for that.

Category 3:

The "need to get a job and keep it, 'cause I ain't feeding you" man. Need I say more? ☺

Category 4:

"Roy". *A category all to himself.*

Roy was licensed to minister after we met. We shared some common ground about past relationships, hurts and desires for ministry. Things were nice for a while. Roy and I would study the Word together and seemed to be growing closer. He shared his version of what happened in his previous relationships. I say his version because a friend of mine once told me that there are three sides to every story. Your side, my side and the truth. So I didn't take sides or try to make any determination about who was right or wrong concerning the other women that had been in his life. What really got my attention though were things he shared about his childhood. What kind of things, you ask? *I'm not going into it. That's not mine to tell.* I also noticed that he was prone to sudden and extreme mood swings. There were times when he'd flip like a pancake! *From nice to nasty in 0.2 seconds.* As time went on, his temper and need for <u>control</u> became unbearable. He and I argued more in 6 months of dating than I had in eight years of marriage with my former husband. I mean loud, threatening and ugly arguments. Absolute nonsense! I was not accustomed to that neither was I going to have my children subjected to abuse from him. I asked him to consider taking an anger management class but he refused. By that time though, I knew this relationship was not going to work. *If you need a class to teach you how to treat me then you are not the one.*

I realized much later that Roy was more typical of what's going on with church folk than I knew. He was moving and functioning in the church but losing in life. He had a church image and then there was the hurting and confused little boy inside of him still throwing periodic temper tantrums to gain the control and attention of those around him. *He was hurting and in turn, hurting others.* Too many of us have been programmed to merely *function* under clouds of depression, guilt, etc.

I had the opportunity to hear Roy speak on several occasions. More than once he talked about Mephibosheth.[11] Although someone else's actions were the cause of his condition, he was still in Lodebar – a place of (emotional) lack, nothingness. *He's not the only one.* We're jumpin', shoutin' and speakin' in tongues, but oh so empty. We look godly, but by holding onto junk that Jesus died to destroy, we are denying His power.[12] I would venture to say that for most of us, the origin of our pain is due to no fault of our own. Mephibosheth had no control over being dropped.[13] We had no control over being molested, raped, rejected or misused. The perpetuation of that pain, however, is within our complete control.

The King has called for you. It's time to pack your bags and crawl, if you must, on out of Lodebar.[14]

Since my Uzziah experience, I've been doing periodic personal assessments. I look at where I've been. Am I heading in the same direction since the last assessment? If yes, why? If no, why not? Every now and then it's just good to de-junk. During each self-assessment I always see mistakes. Some little ones and some huge whopper joppers. Every now and then I see one or two successes. I always find areas in my spiritual life that need to be strengthened. What has been constant is my praise and worship. Not my church praise. No, sometimes you can't fully "open it up" in church. The program says Praise and Worship but it really means song service. *There is a difference.* I'm referring here to my real at home, in the floor, snot-slinging praise and worship. My time in Okinawa had left me with an insatiable desire to learn more about praise and worship and <u>do</u> it. That desire leads me to more Word study, fasting and prayer. I think I have a favorite Psalm for every situation I've been through. I am inspired by the ministries of powerful worship leaders such as Kathryn Kuhlman, Janny Grein, Terry Law and others. My desire to be a pure worshipper compels me to try much harder to treat people right. I can't curse you and bless God with the same mouth.[15] *Hmmm.* This particular assessment revealed that, although I've thrown some pity parties over the years, I had managed to host some powerful personal praise parties as well. In fact, my praise outweighs the bad. The seed planted on that tiny Pacific island has been growing. *Must have fallen on good ground.*

With Roy's departure from my life, it was once again, assessment time. Of course, I recognized the 'woulda, coulda, shouldas' and a small part of me began to think I was my biggest problem as far as relationships were concerned. Maybe, just maybe, I had set the bar unrealistically high. I remember telling Roy that whatever he was dealing with, I was not equipped or willing to deal with. Maybe I just didn't have what was needed to sustain and nurture that relationship – or any relationship. Maybe I was going to miss my blessing (or had already missed it) simply because I wasn't willing to work with a brother. *Am I growing bitter?* Another broken heart. More shattered dreams. *Still got a praise, though.* How many hearts and dreams are allotted per person per lifetime?

Surely I must have reached my quota by now.

Years passed. Look at the time! I'm getting older. The children are growing up. I had wanted so much for them to live in a loving, stable Christian home so that they could really see how a husband and wife should treat each other and work together in life and ministry. Why could "everybody else" find someone to share their life with? I couldn't even find my list of desired traits and qualities for my mate by now. It *had* to be me. Whatever.

Who's Afraid of the Big, Bad Wolf?

Every affliction that comes upon us is not caused by the devil. Sometimes we are drawn away of our own lust.[16] *The basis for which can probably be found in our patterns of wrong thinking.* At other times, God will order a wilderness experience for His divine purpose. Whatever the cause, whatever the affliction my God is able to deliver the righteous out of them all.[17]

"Jonathan" and I officially met in the fall of 2003. We were introduced by a mutual acquaintance. My attraction to him was not looks, money or passion. I liked the fact that we could talk for hours about everything including the scriptures, politics and current events. I hate to admit that even at my age, I can be a little naïve. I assume that because I deal straightforward with people, that others do the same. I'm not a salesman and I don't try to impress. I have never, neither do I have plans to clean, cook or eat a chitterling. I've been broke, busted and disgusted (*most often all at the same time*), I love taking care of my home and family but I don't cook everyday and I am not a slave to a vacuum cleaner. I don't try to mislead anyone about who I am or what I stand for.

Jonathan presented himself as a hard working Christian man. He admitted that he'd made some mistakes (*who hasn't?*) but his desire was to settle down and fulfill the call on his life. He was a licensed and ordained minister; confident, intelligent and serious. He said that he had not had the opportunity to experience a happy family life, neither as a child nor as an adult. He wanted that more than anything and even acted out the part for a while. We talked about our individual memories and experiences of growing up and going to church – me following my daddy and Jonathan with his siblings to hear his mother sing. We spoke detail about some of the family and generational strongholds we saw in both our lives. It was important to me that we put these things on the table. I knew my struggles in dealing with my own and believed what Jonathan said about dealing with his. What were his issues? *I'm not going into it. That's not mine to tell.* I was thankful that I'd finally met someone who acknowledged generational curses and was working to destroy and live above the affects in his life. It seemed that we were of the same mind-set with regards to building and living a Kingdom life together. I was looking forward to building, ministry and a powerful testimony with this man.

One evening, Jonathan came over and we fell asleep on the sofa watching TV. He woke up panicked. He asked if I had opened the door to the laundry room. I had not moved from the chair. He sort of mumbled, "I'm sure that door was closed when I fell to sleep." Although I was a little surprised at how bothered he was about the door, I didn't give it much thought. That was innocent enough. Soon after the "door" incident, he began to complain about lower back pain but he dismissed it as anything serious saying that he had probably hurt it at work. He would ask me to rub and massage his back to ease his "pain". We continued spending a great deal of time together, working, planning, talking and attending church.

We scheduled the wedding for late December. Most of the day before was spent handling our separate last minute details. I had hoped that we would be able to have a late dinner with the kids after all the running around was complete, but Jonathan said that after he finished his errands, he was going to just have some down time. I didn't question him. *What's a relationship without trust?*

The wedding day arrived. Family, friends and on-lookers gathered to witness our vows. My new husband made a lovely speech about how thankful he was for his beautiful new family. We had not planned an elaborate honeymoon, just a few days at the beach to relax. Since we were tired after all of the wedding day festivities we decided to stop for the night mid way. All was well during the wedding night. *Or so I thought.* As we were getting dressed the next morning, Jonathan panicked while looking for his toiletry bag. He was sure he'd packed it. After searching for a few minutes, he looked me square in my eyes and said, "Did you open that door last night and let someone in here? They must have taken my bag!" *Why would I open a hotel room door in the middle of our wedding night and let someone in to take his toiletry bag? Uhhhh...? I didn't know what else to say.* After he found it, right where he'd put it, there was no apology or mention of that episode ever again. We finished dressing and continued on our trip.

While driving, Jonathan talked about how excited and thankful he was that God had given him a wonderful family and another chance to be the husband and father that he should. He said he'd spent the evening before thinking about just that and he asked me not to be mad with him if he told me where he'd gone the evening before. I wasn't mad but puzzled when he confessed that he drove to the beach on Friday evening, the day before Saturday (*which was the day we had planned to go there anyway. Why?*). He said he just wanted to drive and think and have some quiet time. *Cool......right?*

We did a lot of walking and talking while at the beach. Jonathan talked a little about his back again but said it must have had something to do with the way he'd slept. On our last night there, we both fell asleep in the bedroom area of the suite, I awoke during the night and Jonathan was no longer in bed with me. I went to the living room area and the door was locked. I knocked and knocked. No response. I knew that he was a sound sleeper so I finally went back to bed. In the morning, I asked why he'd gone to the other room. He said that he woke up during the night, decided to watch television and since he didn't want to disturb me, he went into the other area. The door must have locked accidentally when he closed it. *Hmmm. It could happen.* A logical, and well thought out answer, but it never settled with me.

Sleeping With The Enemy

Immediately after our return from the wedding trip, Jonathan changed drastically. He became <u>very</u> <u>controlling</u> and began making perverted sexual requests.[18] The requests, he said, were just that – requests. It would be okay if I didn't want to do it. In all the talking and sharing we had done prior to getting married, this had not come up before. I was not comfortable with what he asked so I told him to let me think about it. My years of wondering and wandering have taught me to consult the Word on <u>every</u> area of my life. So I began to search the scriptures.[19] *How could this "man of God" fix his mouth to even ask such a thing?* I thought well if he doesn't bring it up again, I won't. The next day, he asked again. When I told him that not only had I thought about it but I had searched to find out what the Word had to say, he reminded me that the scriptures also state the marriage bed is undefiled. *Hmmm, not <u>my</u> interpretation of that passage.* He seemed to be searching my face, looking for a "break". *I shall <u>not</u> be moved.* He relented, saying that it was only a request and since I obviously was not comfortable with it, we could just forget about it. *Okay, let me do a little damage control here. I would not suggest that any woman challenge her husband's authority or use scriptures to try and justify <u>wrong</u> actions. Let's keep it in context.* ☺

After that, <u>every</u>thing was a problem for Jonathan. He couldn't sleep. He only wanted certain things to eat. He would never clearly communicate what the problem was. During conversation, he would ramble, unlike the straightforward and confident man I'd

met. He began to "misplace" things more often. One night, he heard a car going down the road playing loud music. It sounded as if he mumbled, "they must be trying to send a signal to somebody." *Hmmm.* *You've <u>got</u> to be kidding.* Things seemed to be worse for him at night. He made mention of a bad dream relating to an experience he'd had while living overseas some years earlier. He was not clear about it but he just couldn't find any rest.

I remember waking up a few nights to find him sitting in a chair next to the bed. He'd say nothing was wrong, really. He was just having a little trouble getting to sleep. No problem. Then he started waking me every morning around 3:00 a.m. to pray because *something* was troubling him and he wanted his wife to pray with him. After about a week of that I asked him not to wake me in the middle of the night again. *Maybe all of his newly exposed quirks and need for total control was beginning to wear on me.* I reminded him that our God neither slumbers nor sleeps and I sincerely believed that if he let go of whatever that bad experience had been that he could move past this "thing". I encouraged him to talk about it – maybe even see a counselor. He didn't want to talk about the dream anymore. He was now more concerned with the fact that I didn't want him to wake me up in the wee hours of the morning. We continued to discuss the situation and his demeanor became very nasty. I let him know, *(complete with a "neck roll")*, that I wasn't able to receive his tone of voice. Imagine my surprise to learn that, according to Jon, since he was my "husband now", he could speak to me in any way that he felt God had ordained for him to do so. *Oh really?* I managed to chill. I knew that my role as a single mother for so long had probably hardened me a little. I was not accustomed to having a man in the house and doing things his way. *I'll take that... this time.*

A couple of days later, when I picked Jonathan up from work, he said that he needed to make a stop before going home. He drove to a hotel and while sitting in the parking lot, he announced that he was leaving me "for a season". He said God had spoke to him and said that it was necessary so that we could figure out why he continued to have this "pain". What pain? The pain in his back. I was floored. Why had he not mentioned before now that the pain continued and was more severe? Is it necessary to leave your new wife at home alone (on New Year's Eve) because of a back ache? What's going on here, really? My mind began to race, piecing together previous conversations trying to figure out if there was another woman. *That didn't fit.* What came to my mind was things like him questioning me about why did I "jingle my keys" when I took them out of my purse. "Who was that person you just made eye contact with?" Are you sure you locked the back door when we came in?" Things that, when observed individually, would seem trivial. All of those things and this present episode just didn't add up. *My goodness man, what in the world are you talkin' 'bout?*

I cried, prayed and began to fast. Jonathan would not receive phone calls from me at the hotel but he wrote me a couple of letters and mailed them to the house. *Is he crazy?* He wrote on and on about the pain that I was causing him. 'Why did I lie to him? We have to get beyond the pain'. It sounded as if he was reliving something he had experienced with someone else....some<u>place</u> else. *Was Jonathan dealing with suppressed memory of a traumatic experience?* During all of this, I didn't talk with very many people about what was going on. I had no use for anybody's opinion, good or bad. I confided in a select few friends who stood with me in prayer and emotional support. *Is this demonic activity?* I continued to search the scriptures. To be honest, I didn't like what I finding, so I kept crying, fasting and praying, hoping God would change His answer – *for my comfort, of course.*

I have compared my journal notes with my Bible markings, and realize how clearly and lovingly God carried me through some difficult days and months. He is a very present help in the time of trouble. Look very carefully with me and see The Master's footprints throughout the next few pages.

January 1, 2004 – Isaiah 42:16
I will lead the blind by ways they have not known, along unfamiliar paths I will guide them; I will turn the darkness into light before them and make the rough places smooth. I will not forsake them.

I do believe that everything is spiritual before it becomes physical. I don't care what happens in this earthly realm, it happened first in the spirit realm. I called a couple of pastors and asked for their help through prayer and counseling. No disrespect intended, but they didn't seem to know as much as I did about spiritual warfare. Maybe they just didn't want to get involved. *If you're a child of God, you're already involved.* I wanted to believe my husband was suffering with a mental illness. That, to me, would be no different than if he had a cold or cancer. It was a sickness and I, as his wife, was duty bound to pray for and stand with him, whether he was in the house or not. *That's what I wanted to believe it was.* If only I knew for sure.... I held onto what I did know. I told the devil, "Not this time, buddy. I recognize you." I claimed the authority in the name of Jesus. Satan, the Blood is against you. *Lord, I'm asking you to work it out. Bring Jonathan home.*

January 3, 2004 – Ephesians 6:16-20

In addition to all this, take up the shield of faith, with which you can extinguish all the flaming arrows of the evil one. Take the helmet of salvation and the sword of the Spirit, which is the word of God. And pray in the Spirit on all occasions with all kinds of prayers and requests. With this in mind, be alert and always keep on praying for all the saints. Pray also for me, that whenever I open my mouth, words may be given me so that I will fearlessly make known the mystery of the gospel, for which I am an ambassador in chains. Pray that I may declare it fearlessly, as I should.

January 3, 2004 – Isaiah 28:8-10

All the tables are covered with vomit and there is not a spot without filth. Who is it he is trying to teach? To whom is he explaining his message? To children weaned from their milk, to those just taken from the breast? For it is: Do and do, do and do, rule on rule, rule on rule, a little here, a little there.

I knew that I had to seek wise and Godly counsel on this matter from people experienced in spiritual warfare. And I needed to be where I didn't know anybody and they didn't know me – no preconceived notions on either side. I pressed my way to a ministry out of our area. The Spirit of the Lord spoke encouragement and confirmation through the Bishop and the Pastor.

January 4, 2004 – Isaiah 41:18-20

I will make rivers flow on barren heights, and springs within the valleys. I will turn the desert into pools of water, and the parched ground into springs. I will put in the desert the cedar and the acacia, the myrtle and the olive. I will set pines in the wasteland, the fir and the cypress together, so that people may see and know, may consider and understand, that the hand of the Lord has done this, that the Holy One of Israel has created it.

Okay, God I understand that you are going to do some supernatural things with this situation so that everybody will know that only You could have done it but I'm still not clear on exactly what I'm dealing with. I prayed to God – expose and reveal.

Very shortly after that – maybe a couple nights later, I saw in a dream, Jonathan being pinned to the ground, face down by a nude male figure. I only saw a rear view of the figure and the portion of Jonathan's face I saw was twisted in pain and he was struggling to free himself. I was convinced that *something* had happened to him early in life to trigger his present behavior. If only he would deal with it then let it go, we could overcome this attack of the enemy.

January 9, 2004 – Psalms 34:4
I sought the LORD, and he answered me, and delivered me from all my fears.

A house divided against itself can not stand. Once Jonathan started receiving my calls, I told him that whatever he had been dealing with now affected me and that we should stand together. He returned home on January 9th.

It was a Friday night. He began to talk more about some of his childhood and young adult experiences. Finally, I had started to listen to what the Word of God was saying to me and I was now paying attention to the red flags. Jonathan's "stories" now centered around "somebody did something" to him. He would never say what. Remembering my dream, I asked if he'd been molested as a child. He said no, but it was almost as if he was trying to tell me enough of *something* so that I'd figure out the rest and help him. Or he was playing some sort of cat and mouse game. We talked almost all night. He seemed sincere about wanting to get to the bottom of whatever the problem might be.

On that Saturday night Jonathan was adamant about driving to North Carolina to attend a revival service at his brother's church. It was a strange trip. Jonathan had insisted on packing some snacks and a couple of blankets. I suggested that we just plan to stay overnight. He didn't want to do that. I put my purse in the car before we left, but when we stopped for gas, I couldn't find it. . *Hmmm. Where is it?* On the drive there Jonathan pointed out an area that he said was known for witch activity. *No real point. Just casual conversation.* He talked about different events in his childhood, going more into detail. Some of the stories now sounded a little bizarre. He'd talked before about some church experiences, now his posture and tone displayed an obvious contempt, even hatred for people of God. It began to sound as if Jonathan had a problem with any spiritual authority that tried to correct or counsel him.[20] Some of the people he'd previously spoken highly of, he now seemed to want to discredit or blemish their reputation.[21] *Why?* After the service I noticed that this brother and sister-in-law were not friendly at all. They barely even spoke to us. It was almost as if we had the plague. *Who were they avoiding – really?* I was beginning to think that Jonathan's family issues had gone much deeper than he'd said.

On the drive home Jonathan shared with me what he believed was <u>our</u> "problem". Me. According to him, I was the direct reason for his "pain". He said I was getting up at night, moving him around and molesting him while he slept through it all. He said that he could only remember things in bits and pieces but he was sure that I used some type of "hold" that I must have learned in the military to put him to sleep. "Just like that night we were watching TV", he said. "Either you did something then or you let somebody in and they did it." *Say what!?* He also told me that he didn't sleep at night because he'd trained himself to stay awake between 2 a.m. and 5 a.m. because - - - well, that's when witches do most of their "work". *Go on and say it "Hmmm".* (I have a couple of theories about his obsession with witches and people coming in the house at night to "get" him – *but that's another book*.) When we got home, after the long trip and the exhausting conversation, I was numb. What did all his ramblings mean? I found the purse that I know I had put in the car before we left. It was on the bed carefully covered with a blanket. *How did it get there?*

I don't know that I slept at all that night.

Why me? All I wanted was to have a normal married life – a family. Is that wrong? Is that too much to ask? As I was getting out of bed the next morning – which was Sunday, Jonathan said, "You did it again, you know." *Ugghh!* I was at my wits end. I persuaded him to attend service that day at someone's church whom I knew was a powerful woman of God and also happens to be a professional counselor. She was not expecting us but after the service we were invited into her office for a visit. She and I had not talked previously about what was going on. As we sat together in her office, I told her what Jonathan had said to me the night before. She didn't flinch or bat an eyelash but simply asked him if he had been molested as a child or engaged in any homosexual activity. (I had not had the opportunity to tell her about my dream) His response was a calm, but definitely agitated – "No." Jonathan would not entertain any conversation about himself.[22] He only expressed concern that I get "delivered" from whatever was causing me to hurt him. The conversation started going around in circles so we agreed to return to her office on Tuesday for further counseling.

Although I was now seeing some strange things with Jonathan, I was not afraid of him. That's not to brag. *Maybe I didn't have enough sense to be afraid.* I really wanted him to know that no matter who or what had hurt him in the past, I was willing and able to stand with him. We could break this thing. We went to work as usual on Monday morning (January 11th) and met for lunch. During lunch, Jonathan was not interested in talking about his "pain", or what might be discovered during the scheduled counseling session. He was now upset because it had just occurred to him that I had never even offered to add his name to my property. *You really are crazy. Aren't you?* ☺ I reminded him that we had talked about property and debts prior to getting married and were in agreement with current arrangements and future plans. *Guess he had forgotten.*

Jonathan called me at my office about 2:00 p.m. to let me know that he had gone back to the house and gotten his things. He just couldn't live with the "pain". I had prayed earnestly, anointed the house and cast out any and everything that would attempt to exalt itself against my God. Why did Jonathan leave again? Why could he not "rest"? *God, how could You allow this to happen? I asked You to work it out and bring Jon home – to stay.* **Do you** *want Jon home or do you want Me to work it out? The two are not necessarily the same.*

January 13, 2004 – 2 Thessalonians 2:1-3
Concerning the coming of our Lord Jesus Christ and our being gathered together to be with Him, we ask you, brothers, not to become easily unsettled or alarmed by some prophecy, report or letter supposed to have come from us, saying that the day of the Lord has already come. Don't let anyone deceive you in any way, for that day will not come, until the rebellion occurs and the man of lawlessness is revealed, the man doomed to destruction.

January 15, 2004 – Jude v 4, 20-25
For certain men whose condemnation was written about long ago have secretly slipped in among you. They are godless men, who change the grace of our God into a license for immorality and deny Jesus Christ our only Sovereign and Lord.

But you, dear friends, build yourselves up in your most holy faith and pray in the Holy Spirit. Keep yourselves in God's love as you wait for the mercy of our Lord Jesus Christ to bring you to eternal life. Be merciful to those who doubt; snatch others from the fire and save them; to others show mercy, mixed with fear – hating even the clothing stained by corrupted flesh.

January 16, 2004 – 2 Corinthians 10:3-5
For though we live in the world, we do not wage war as the world does. The weapons we fight with are not the weapons of the world, on the contrary, they have divine power to demolish strongholds.

January 17, 2004 – 1 Peter 2:19-20
For it is commendable if a man bears up under the pain of unjust suffering because he is conscious of God. But how is it to your credit if you receive a beating for doing wrong and endure it? But if you suffer for doing good and you endure it, this is commendable before God.

January 18, 2004 – 1 Peter 4:19
So then, those who suffer according to God's will should commit themselves to their faithful Creator and continue to do good.

January 20, 2004 – 2 Corinthians 4:8-9
We are hard pressed on every side, but not crushed; perplexed, but not abandoned; struck down, but not destroyed.

About a week after Jonathan left the house for the last time, I got a call from the Sheriff's department asking me to come to their office to respond to accusations of criminal domestic violence and sexual assault. *You must have the wrong number.* As I sat in the investigator's office and read "the accuser's" account of the assault, I was flabbergasted.[23] His story was detailed, demonstrating a thorough thought process. He wrote about jingling keys, cars sending signals as they drove down the road. He was elaborate about how I would use some type of military hold to put him to sleep. Once he was out, I would move him to various positions, molest him, wash, dry and replace the linen then put him back to bed before morning. *I don't do that much all day.* I was very surprised to learn from this report that he had been going to the doctor for many weeks complaining that he thought I was abusing him during the night. *Hmpf. All this time, I've been worrying the Lord about how to help Jon and he's been conjuring up mess!*

Wait a minute. If Jonathan was taking his current lie to this level, flip flopping the characters and trying to make people believe that I was the villain, then what about the things he had said about his past? *Had he been orchestrating a devious mind game from the beginning?*[24] This foolishness didn't just start. He's too detailed. Too slippery. Jonathan's been dealing with this issue for a long time. *Somethin' in the milk ain't clean.*

Okay, I can be honest with you, right? When Jonathan left the second time, I continued to cry, fast and pray just like I said but I also did a little detective work. *I sometimes think that's my true calling.* With the help of some very resourceful friends, I found phone numbers and addresses for people who had been a part of Jonathan's life over the years and I called or emailed (sometimes both) them all. I had a lot of questions. Some of them did not even respond. Some that did respond tried not to have a lot of answers. What they didn't say (or do) was more revealing than what they did say. I had learned enough about Jonathan to know that his procedure was not to completely fabricate a story. He would exaggerate details, omit information and confuse the characters' behaviors and actions. So when his family said that they had NO idea of what was going on with him, I didn't believe them. *Why do we keep trying to hide that big ole dragon in the closet when we need to just slay him?* I found it interesting though that about five out of the six people I did talk to asked if I was alright. They wanted to know if he had hurt me. *Hmmm.* During this time, Jonathan wrote me another letter about how he just "can't live with the pain". *Puhleese stop wastin' up all this paper writin' letters!*

A friend and I drove to North Carolina and pulled some public records looking for answers. What I found led to more questions. So I did more searching, made more phone calls. As it turned out, more of my suspicions were confirmed. Jonathan did not have a problem talking about things that had happened in his life he just didn't put the characters or sequence of events in the right order. *Can you turn "crazy" off and on like a faucet?* I've since heard the term 'transference' used to describe what he was doing. It's like he was living in a pseudo world, close to reality but with his own twist to things.

Although I learned that Jonathan had lied about many, many, many things....okay, practically everything, I was more disappointed than angry. Now I was more concerned about the condition of his soul than our marriage.

The Sheriff's department had to investigate his complaint. Nothing came together. The doctor could not find any evidence of abuse. *Duh? There was no abuse.* His charges were thrown out as was his request for a restraining order against me. *Just like my DADDY – marched from judgement hall to judgement hall.* Friends pleaded with me to request a restraining order against Jonathan. I refused to do so. A lot of dead people had a restraining order in place besides, "the Lord knows how to deliver the godly..."[25] I had slept in the same bed with the enemy, I mean Jonathan. If he were able to hurt me, he would have done it then.

It would be too much for me to explain every piece of information that I learned about Jonathan. In addition to that, I have no desire to <u>unnecessarily</u> offend him or his family. I provided an outline to the Investigator of some things Jonathan had told me along with documentation of the facts. *Look at his pattern of twisting information. Am I the only one who sees how desperately he needs help? Can't somebody do something to help him before he hurts someone? If he hasn't already.*

The next few months were a blur working and trying to maintain a normal home life with the children. Add to that more interviews with the Sheriff's department, my attorney and of course the nosey questions and wondering stares. I don't know that I ever fully appreciated Christ's crucifixion until now. It was more than the physical pain of the beatings and thorns on His head. It was betrayal at the hand of someone who was supposed to be showing love. It was the mocking and removal of His covering[26] to allow public exposure of what should never have been seen by any and every body. *Yeah, but if we are crucified with Christ, then......*

February 1, 2004 – 2 Peter 2:1, 9-15
False prophets appeared in the past among the people and in the same way false teachers will appear among you. They will secretly introduce

destructive heresies, even denying the sovereign Lord who bought them – bringing swift destruction on themselves.

So, then the Lord knows how to rescue the godly men from trials and to hold the unrighteous for the day of judgement, while continuing their punishment. This is especially true of those who follow the corrupt desire of the sinful nature and despise authority. Bold and arrogant, these men are not afraid to slander celestial beings; yet even angels, although they are stronger and more powerful, do not bring slanderous accusations against such beings in the presence of the Lord. But these men blaspheme in matters they do not understand. They are like brute beasts, creatures of instinct, born only to be caught and destroyed, and like beasts they too will perish. They will be paid back with harm for the harm they have done. Their idea of pleasure is to carouse in broad daylight. They are blots and blemishes, reveling in their pleasures while they feast with you. With eyes full of adultery, they never stop sinning; they seduce the unstable, they are experts in greed – an accursed brood! They have left the straightway and wandered off to follow the way of Balaam son of Beor, who loved the wages of wickedness.

February 1, 2004 – Isaiah 41:11-13

All who rage against you will surely be ashamed and disgraced; those who oppose you will be as nothing and perish. Though you search for your enemies, you will not find them. Those who wage war against you will be as nothing at all. For I am the Lord, your God, who takes hold of your right hand and says to you, Do not fear; I will help you.

February 1, 2004 – Psalms 37:35-36

I have seen a wicked and ruthless man flourishing like a green tree in its native soil, but he soon passed away and was no more; though I looked for him, he could not be found.

February 7, 2004 – Psalms 27

The Lord is my light and my salvation; whom shall I fear? The LORD is the stronghold of my life; of whom shall I be afraid? When evil men advance against me to devour my flesh, when my enemies and my foes attack me, they stumble and fall. Though an army besiege me, my heart will not fear; though war break out against me, even then will I be confident. One thing I ask of the Lord, this is what I seek: that I may dwell in the house of the Lord all the days of my life, to gaze upon the beauty of the Lord and to seek him in his temple. For in the day of trouble he will keep me safe in his dwelling;

he will hide me in the shelter of his tabernacle and set me high upon a rock. Then my head will be exalted above the enemies who surround me; at his tabernacle will I sacrifice with shouts of joy; I will sing and make music to the Lord. Hear my voice when I call, O Lord; be merciful to me and answer me. My heart says of you, "Seek his face!" Your face, Lord, I will seek. Do not hide your face from me, do not turn your servant away in anger; you have been my helper. Do not reject me or forsake me, O God my Savior. Though my father and mother forsake me, the Lord will receive me. Teach me your way, O Lord; lead me in a straight path because of my oppressors. Do not turn me over to the desire of my foes, for false witnesses rise up against me, breathing out violence. I am still confident of this: I will see the goodness of the Lord in the land of the living. Wait for the Lord; be strong and take heart and wait for the Lord.

February 8, 2004 – 2 Timothy 3: 8-12

Just as Jannes and Jambres opposed Moses, so also these men oppose the truth – men of depraved minds, who, as far as the faith is concerned, are rejected. But they will not get very far because, as in the case of those men, their folly will be clear to everyone. You, however, know all about my teaching, my way of life, my purpose, faith, patience, love, endurance, persecutions, sufferings – what kinds of things happened to me in Antioch, Iconium and Lystra, the persecutions I endured. Yet the Lord rescued me from all of them. In fact, everyone who wants to live a godly life in Christ Jesus will be persecuted.

It was only after one of my counselors spoke it to me that I could accept that fact I would not be able to help Jonathan. He <u>chose</u> not to be helped. *I will dance out my clothes in praise before my God but I will not lose another minute's rest fooling with Jonathan and no demons!*

February 17, 2004 – 1 John 5:16
If anyone sees his brother commit a sin that does not lead to death, he should pray and God will give him life. I refer to those whose sin does not lead to death. There is a sin that leads to death. I am not saying that he should pray about that.

February 18, 2004 – Matthew 18:7-8
Woe to the world because of the things that cause people to sin! Such things must come, but woe to the man through whom they come! If your hand or your foot causes you to sin, cut it off and throw it away. It is better for you to enter life maimed or

crippled than to have two hands or two feet and be thrown into eternal fire.

February 18, 2004 – Hebrews 6:1-8
Therefore let us leave the elementary teachings about Christ and go on to maturity, not laying again the foundation of repentance from acts that lead to death, and of faith in God, instruction about baptisms, the laying on of hands, the resurrection of the dead, and eternal judgment. And God permitting, we will do so. It is impossible for those who have once been enlightened, who have tasted the heavenly gift, who have shared in the Holy Spirit, who have tasted the goodness of the word of God and the powers of the coming age, if they fall away, to be brought back to repentance, because to their loss they are crucifying the Son of God all over again and subjecting him to public disgrace. Land that drinks in the rain often falling on it and that produces a crop useful to those for whom it is farmed receives the blessing of God. But land that produces thorns and thistles is worthless and is in danger of being cursed. In the end it will be burned.

February 19, 2004 – Acts 13:6-10
They traveled through the whole island until they

came to Paphos. There they met a Jewish sorcerer and false prophet named Bar-Jesus, who was an attendant of the proconsul, Sergius Paulus. The proconsul, an intelligent man, sent for Barnabas and Saul because he wanted to hear the word of God. But Elymas the sorcerer (for that is what his name means) opposed them and tried to turn the proconsul from the faith. Then Saul, who was also called Paul, filled with the Holy Spirit, looked straight at Elymas and said, "You are a child of the devil and an enemy of everything that is right! You are full of all kinds of deceit and trickery. Will you never stop perverting the right ways for the Lord?"

I requested an annulment of the marriage.[27] Some would say that it didn't work because we didn't date long enough. There wasn't enough time for me to really know him. I say, "Phooey!" Jonathan had enough time to lie.

March 10, 2004 – Psalm 34:9-22
Fear the Lord, you his saints, for those who fear him lack nothing. The lions may grow weak and hungry, but those who seek the Lord lack no good thing. Come my children, listen to me; I will teach you the fear of the Lord. Whoever of you loves life

and desires to see many good days, keep your tongue from evil and your lips from speaking lies. Turn from evil and do good; seek peace and pursue it. The eyes of the Lord are on the righteous and his ears are attentive to their cry; the face of the Lord is against those who do evil, to cut off the memory of them from the earth. The righteous cry out, and the Lord hears them; he delivers them from all their troubles. The Lord is close to the brokenhearted and saves those who are crushed in spirit. A righteous man may have many troubles but the Lord delivers him from them all; he protects all his bones, not one of them will be broken. Evil will slay the wicked; the foes of the righteous will be condemned. The Lord redeems his servants; no one will be condemned who takes refuge in him.

March 13, 2004 – Psalms 35

Contend, O Lord, with those who contend with me; fight against those who fight against me. Take up shield and buckler; arise and come to my aid. Brandish spear and javelin against those who pursue me. Say to my soul, "I am your salvation." May those who seek my life be disgraced and put to shame; may those who plot my ruin be turned back in dismay. May they be like chaff before the wind, with the angel of the Lord driving them away; may their path be dark and slippery, with the angel of the

Lord pursuing them. Since they hid their net for me without cause and without cause dug a pit for me, may ruin overtake them by surprise – may the net they hid entangle them, may they fall into the pit, to their ruin. Then my soul will rejoice in the Lord and delight in his salvation. My whole being will exclaim, "Who is like you, O Lord? You rescue the poor from those too strong for them, the poor and needy from those who rob them." Ruthless witnesses come forward; they question me on things I know nothing about. They repay me evil for good and leave my soul forlorn. Yet when they were ill, I put on sackcloth and humbled myself with fasting. When my prayers returned unanswered, I went about mourning as though for my friend or brother. I bowed my head in grief as though weeping for my mother. But when I stumbled, they gathered in glee; attackers gathered against me when I was unaware. They slandered me without ceasing. Like the ungodly they maliciously mocked; they gnashed their teeth at me. O Lord, how long will you look on? Rescue my life from their ravages, my precious life from these lions. I will give you thanks in the great assembly; among throngs of people I will praise you. Let not those gloat over me who are my enemies without cause; let not those who hate me without reason maliciously wink the eye. They do not speak peaceably, but devise false accusations against those who live quietly in the land. They

*gape at me and say, "Aha! Aha! With our own eyes
we have seen it." O Lord, you have seen this; be not
silent. Do not be far from me, O Lord. Awake, and
rise to my defense! Contend for me, my God and
Lord. Vindicate me in your righteousness,
O Lord my God; do not let them think, "Aha, just
what we wanted!" or say, "We have swallowed him
up." May all who gloat over my distress be put to
shame and confusion; may all who exalt themselves
over me be clothed with shame and disgrace. May
those who delight in my vindication shout for joy
and gladness; may they always say, "The Lord be
exalted, who delights in the well-being of his
servant." My tongue will speak of your
righteousness and of your praises all day long.*

While waiting for the court date, I received a
copy of a letter that had been written by- guess
who - Jonathan two days before we married.
Another letter. He had mailed it to someone
back home and they felt the need to share it
with me.   The letter was full of incoherent
ramblings about him wanting forgiveness for
any wrong he had done to anyone and leaving

all his worldly possessions to his children. He hoped that Jesus would wash him anew in His blood and receive him with open arms. *A suicide letter? Written two days before we married? Hmmm.*

It's hard to describe my feelings as I read that letter. I thought about all the little incidents that didn't make sense separately. I recalled Jonathan telling me that he had gone to the beach alone the day before we planned to go there together. That was just one day after he had written and mailed this letter I was now holding. *Had he gone there to kill himself or to plan how he was going to kill both of us the next day?* I also thought about the night we drove to North Carolina. *Did he hide my purse under that blanket and plan to harm and/or abandon me in an unfamiliar area without money or identification?*

While it did not answer every one of my lingering questions, this little piece of paper put things into perspective for me. There was never a covenant of marriage.

I believe that Jonathan's intention had been to harm or kill me on <u>at least</u> two occasions. But he couldn't. *The angels of the most high God have charge over me.* There was definitely a battle going on. It's like there was more than one person in there – *"legions, baby"*. The good Jon wouldn't let the bad Jon do everything he wanted to do but neither would the bad Jon let the good Jon do everything he wanted to do. The enemy had him and wanted me dead or at the very least, under his <u>control</u>. *Please look again at 2 Timothy 3:1-6.*

I was hurt, disappointed and continued to seek God for answers and deliverance. Call me thorough, *or nosey* but I also continued to conduct my own investigation of Jonathan's background as well. I didn't get the answers I wanted neither did deliverance come the way I expected. *Alas, God is still on the throne and I'm still cute.* ☺ As the dust from all of this drama was settling, I wanted to know why was it that Jonathan and I were not able to break the strongholds. This may sound a little harsh, but my hurt and disappointment had less to do with the dissolution of the marital relationship and more to do with the fact that I felt the enemy had won - again. *I wanted this victory for the Kingdom.* I asked God, "Why?!" He didn't tell me "why" but He told me "stop!" Stop probing into what caused Jonathan to fall away, before I found myself lost in that same darkness. *Focus on the <u>Light</u> and darkness will cease.*

I was sharing a portion of my testimony with a minister friend one day and she asked if I'd read "If He Doesn't Deliver" by Marilyn Joyce. She shared her copy and I read the entire book in one night. ***"It was about choices. <u>You</u> chose to seek My face."*** I'll say it again. Life is all about choices. The simple everyday choices. <u>*Choose*</u> *to focus on the Light.*

April 19, 2004 – Hebrews 10:36-39
You need to persevere so that when you have done the will of God, you will receive what he has promised. For in just a very little while, "He who is coming will come and will not delay. But my righteous one will live by faith. And if he shrinks back, I will not be pleased with him." But we are not of those who shrink back and are destroyed, but of those who believe and are saved.

May 21, 2004 – Galatians 4:1-7

What I am saying is that as long as the heir is a child, he is no different from a slave, although he owns the whole estate. He is subject to guardians and trustees until the time set by his father. So also, when we were children, we were in slavery under the basic principles of the world. But when the time had fully come, God sent his Son, born of a woman, born under law to redeem those under law, that we might receive the full rights of sons. Because you are sons, God sent the Spirit of his Son into our hearts, the Spirit who calls out, "Abba, Father." So you are no longer a slave but a son; and since you are a son, God has made you also an heir.

May 23, 2004 – John 2:1-11

On the third day a wedding took place at Cana in Galilee. Jesus' mother was there, and Jesus and his disciples had also been invited to the wedding. When the wine was gone, Jesus' mother said to him, "They have no more wine." "Dear woman, why do you involve me?" Jesus replied. "My time has not yet come." His mother said the the servants, "Do whatever he tells you." Nearby stood six stone water jars, the kind used by the Jews for ceremonial washing, each holding from twenty to thirty gallons. Jesus said to the servants, "Fill the jars with water"; so they filled them to the brim. Then he told them, "Now draw some out and take it to the master of the banquet." They did so, and the master of the banquet tasted the water that had been turned into wine. He did not realize where it had come from; though the servants who had drawn the water knew. Then he called the bridegroom aside and said, "Everyone brings out the choice wine first and then the cheaper wine after the guests have had too much to drink; but you have saved the best for now." This, the first of his miraculous signs, Jesus performed at Cana in Galilee. He thus revealed his glory and his disciples put their faith in him.

For months, I had to rest in <u>simple</u> trust for God's divine protection of my family and wait. You do NOT want me to get started on how difficult that was. No need to holla, fuss, kick and scream. *Neither God nor demons are moved by such hysterics.*

June 1, 2004 – Joel 2:25-27
I will repay you for the years the locusts have eaten – the great locust and the young locust, the other locusts and the locust swarm – my great army that I sent among you . You will have plenty to eat, until you are full, and you will praise the name of the Lord your God, who has worked wonders for you; never again will my people be shamed. Then you

will know that I am in Israel, that I am the Lord
your God, and that there is no other, never again
will my people be shamed.

June 9, 2004 – Isaiah 41:10-13, 15

So do not fear, for I am with you; do not be
dismayed, for I am your God. I will strengthen you
and help you; I will uphold you with my righteous
right hand. All who rage against you will surely be
ashamed and disgraced; those who oppose you will
be as nothing and perish. Though you search for
your enemies, you will not find them. Those who
wage war against you will be as nothing at all. For
I am the Lord, your God, who takes hold of your
right hand and says to you, Do not fear; I will help
you.

"See, I will make you into a threshing sledge, new
and sharp, with many teeth. You will thresh the
mountains and crush them, and reduce the hills to
chaff."

My request for annulment was granted in June
2004. After all that flappin', scheming and
lying, Jonathan was not even present for the
hearing. Look again at Isaiah 41:11-13,

*All who rage against you will surely be
ashamed and disgraced; those who oppose you
will be as nothing and perish.
<u>Though you search for your enemies you will
not find them.</u> <u>Those who wage war against
you will be as nothing at all</u>.
For I am the Lord, your God, who takes hold of
your right hand and says to you,
Do not fear; I will help you.*

and Psalm 37:35-36.

*I have seen a wicked and ruthless man
flourishing like a green tree in its native soil,
but he soon passed away and was no more;
<u>though I looked for him, he could not be found.</u>*

God <u>CAN NOT</u> lie!

When a Lie Becomes The Truth

Assessment time. Why in the world did I have to go through all of that? *Have I allowed my desire to marry override my pursuit of God? Lord, please forgive me.* Why did Hosea have to marry a whore?[21] Because he had to "live the message" before he could "give the message" to God's people. Please, PUHLEESE hear my message: We are, indeed, living in the last and evil days. Certain things must happen. *No shortcuts* False prophets gotta do their thing but the saints of God <u>must</u> do their thing as well. *No compromise* Your praise, prayer, testimony and fulfillment of duty are not optional.

This is warfare. I ask you – no, I beg you to man your post. We are a peculiar people. We do not fit in. We are not normal. Trying to be normal and ignore what the Word of God was speaking to me could have gotten me killed and passivity is killing the church.

Why,... how could Jon accuse me of such awful and disgusting things?[29] It's hard to understand how he could be so strange, sinister, even evil but maintain employment and hold intelligent conversation (except when asked direct questions about his past). *What is going on here, really?* What I found to be most troubling about the whole thing was that Jonathan seemed to actually believe his own lies. How <u>did</u> the truth get so twisted? *Whew! I thought you'd never ask.*

Do you remember I mentioned, certain scriptures got stuck in my craw and just wouldn't move? That was long before I met Jonathan. At the time, I couldn't comprehend what the Word was saying, and to be honest, the little I did understand was disturbing. So, the good Lord, in His unparalleled wisdom, provided on the job training. *Hmmm. It's humbling – and sometimes quite terrifying - to go from reading the Word to living the Word.*

Romans 1:18-20
The wrath of God is being revealed from heaven against all the godlessness and wickedness of men who suppress the truth by their wickedness, since what may be known about God is plain to them, because God has made it plain to them. For since the creation of the world God's invisible qualities – his eternal power and divine nature – have been clearly seen, being understood from what has been made, so that men are without excuse.

Those who know the truth are holding it back. Why? Perhaps the truth is not popular. Those of us who have a testimony of the power of God must speak up. We absolutely must acknowledge and reverence our heavenly Father.

Romans 1:21-23
For although they knew God, they neither glorified him as God nor gave thanks to him, but their thinking became futile and their foolish hearts were darkened. Although they claimed to be wise, they became fools and exchanged the glory of the

immortal God for images made to look like mortal man and birds and animals and reptiles.

Verses 21-23 greatly concern me. They <u>knew</u> God. These are church folk. I think about how often I hear worship leaders practically beg people to tell God "thank you". To be unthankful is ungodly. But rather than thank God for His wondrous works, we seek to bring the things of God down to the level of man so that it is comfortable for us. How do we do that? With man made doctrine - - our own set of rules.

Romans 1:24-27
Therefore God gave them over in the sinful desires of their hearts to sexual impurity for the degrading of their bodies with one another. They exchanged the truth of God for a lie, and worshiped and served the created things rather than the Creator – who is forever praised. Amen. Because of this, God gave them over to shameful lusts. Even their women exchanged natural relations for unnatural ones. In

the same way the men also abandoned natural relations with women and were inflamed with lust for one another. Men committed indecent acts with other men, and received in themselves the due penalty for their perversion.

The ungodly refuse to glorify God and be thankful. They change the glory of God into an image that man can relate to. *He told 'em plain as day not to do that* So, God took His hands off of them and let them progress *or should I say digress* to other things. They continue to plummet into as much sin as their evil minds can think of and even forsake the natural use of their own bodies.

Romans 1:28
Furthermore, since they did not think it worthwhile to retain the knowledge of God, he gave them over to a depraved mind, to do what ought not to be done.

Did I mention that these were church folk? They heard the Word but would not hold on to it. The reprobate or corrupted mind described in verses 24 through 28 started out in verses 18 through 23 knowing God but <u>not</u> glorifying Him and being unthankful. Somewhere along the line, a decision was made to not glorify God and to not be thankful. As a result, the reprobate will find themselves in a much worse condition than someone who had never been saved.

So, when *does* a lie become truth? When we, who know the truth <u>choose</u> not to tell it. When we who know God <u>choose</u> not to acknowledge or glorify Him as God. When we <u>choose</u> to be unthankful and live unholy.

Hmmm, I feel another letter.

Dear Jon,

I'll get right to the point and express my disappointment with your actions. I asked you time and time again to stop trying to make _me_ "they". Deal with whomever or whatever hurt you then let it go. Maybe it's too painful. It could be too late.

You really tried to show out, didn't you? Oh, but don't fool yourself, God is not mocked. You will see it again. I have wondered (not lately, though) what is the origin of your issues – traumatic experience, mental illness or maybe you opened yourself up to something evil. It is quite possibly, a combination of things. I used to think that you were trying to reveal enough of something so that I'd figure it out and force you to get help. But I've also seen that you are very calculating and quite resourceful. You managed to fraudulently use the resources of the Sheriff's Department, the court system, medical and treatment facilities – all to benefit your sadistic and twisted game. I believe with everything in me that you are hiding much more than what I found and that "thing" is the source of your pain.

I am thankful for the blood of Jesus that covers me and my family. Some people gawk at the situation and say, "What a mess". I, on the other hand, see the awesomeness of my Creator – how He kept me and say, "What a God"! Know that I am neither angry nor bitter. There are no shortcuts in life. This experience with you was necessary. I'm better for it.

I remain, just as you found me,... In His care

Cynthia ~ ~ ~

Okay, I'm about to get an understanding of how this thing works. I will <u>not</u> lay down. I will <u>not</u> die. I do <u>not</u> fit in, I am <u>not</u> normal. "Life" will continue to happen to me. There's no stopping that. I <u>choose</u> to allow "life" to happen <u>through</u> me...*to the glory of the Father.*

Chapter 4: Better

or Bitter

Sadness

Sadness is a feeling of loss,

as Romeo felt for his "dead" Juliet.

Sadness makes you feel empty,

like a dried up well.

Sadness is like a drooping flower,

hoping to straighten up again.

In other words,

"Sadness" is just a pain in the neck.

by Cierra Mitchell

You Have Options

I wish I could say that through all the trials, tribulations, and warfare I have remained upright and chaste. Actually, I could say that but the truth of the matter is I have struggled for years in many areas of my life – relationships, flesh and finances. I've done some things I shouldn't have – didn't do some things I shoulda. There've been heart breaks, tummy aches, set-ups, set-backs, bloopers and blunders. Truth be told, I've thrown in the towel a time or two. But I have <u>chosen</u> not to go out like that – belly up in a defeated rut. More than once, I have had to decide: Lay down and die or get up and fight? It occurred to me only recently that I had never clearly defined what I had been fighting for. Initially, I would have said that I was fighting to preserve and improve my life and that of my children.

Or I would have said that I was fighting not to lose my mind in the craziness around me. Actually, I've been fighting to lose <u>my</u> mind, my <u>old</u> mind and replace it with the mind of Christ. I've had to <u>"move"</u>, my mind first, from where I was – *working in the church* – to Christ's location – *operating in ministry.* From the familiar - *just getting by* – to the anointed - *life more abundantly.* Contentment is a fruit of the Spirit. Complacency, on the other hand, is a fruit of the enemy. There is a difference and I have a choice.

In review, I realize that some of my worst mistakes were made when I felt backed into a corner, rocking and reeling from a recently inflicted pain...when I didn't think I had a choice....when I couldn't see the options. Once you initiate the "move" in your mind, there comes a time when you realize that sadness really is "just a pain in the neck". *Out of the mouth of babes.* <u>Choose</u> not to keep your focus there. One of my favorite passages of scripture might help. James 1:2[1] does not say that it <u>is</u> all joy. It says that we are to <u>count</u> it all joy. Not some of it but all of it. It may be unavoidable that I pass through the valley of the shadow of death, - *There are no shortcuts* - but I don't have to stay there. It's my decision.

It's assessment time. *Okay work with me for a minute.* We're going to complete a little exercise. We will start with two sheets of paper then you get to <u>choose</u> which one you will keep once we're done. Do you have your two sheets of paper and a pen? At the top of one sheet write the word "joy" and on the other sheet write "junk". Now, start with the "joy" sheet and list every good thing that has ever happened to you. Don't forget about that promotion, your peace of mind and how calm traffic was on your way home from work today. Count each item listed and write that number next to the word "joy" at the top of your paper. Now, let's work with the "junk" sheet. *Go get a box of kleenex. Take your time, I'll wait.* List every negative experience you can remember happened to you. Include that time you got fired, the traffic jam on your way to work this morning and when your dog died. Alright let's tally. Write the total number of "junk" items at the top of your paper labeled "junk". Reflect. As you thought about and listed those "junk" items, how did it feel? Was it pleasant reliving those things for the past few minutes? At this point, can you change any of those "junk" items? Would it be worth it?

Do you really want to replay those hurts over and over in your mind…day after day….month after month….year after year? Which list do you prefer to keep? If you say the "joy" list, then take the final number you came up with from the "junk" list and add that to the number you listed on the "joy" sheet. Now throw the "junk" sheet in the nearest trash receptacle. If you prefer holding on to the "junk" list then stop reading, close this book and throw it in the nearest trash receptacle. If you haven't decided which you'd rather hold onto, keep reading.

Why did I choose to share my story with you, particularly my experiences with Roy and Jonathan? To demonstrate the three choices you were just given. I believe Roy, at the time I knew him, was still holding onto both pieces of paper. Undecided. I honestly don't think he *wanted* to be lame – he probably didn't even realize it. *We can be broken so long until we can't even imagine what it's like to be fixed.* Jon, I fear, was holding tightly onto the "junk" sheet. He'd thrown away the "joy" list (*and kicked over the trash can*). Me? I've got JOY and I'm still reading the Book. ☺

We've got to <u>decide</u> that as believers of God, we are either going to lay down and die or get up and fight. Please notice that I did not say we are believers <u>in</u> God. I know you believe <u>in</u> God. *That's why you put on them tight shoes and go to church every Sunday.* ☺ You've got to decide if you <u>believe</u> God. Do you take Him at His Word? If no, then lay down. If yes, then act on it. Consider, if you will, the four lepers in 2 Kings Chapter 7.[2] Now, there's a pitiful picture. As lepers they were already outcasts and unwanted. Add to that, they are about to starve to death. If they stayed where they were, they would <u>surely</u> die. If they ventured away from familiar territory, they <u>might</u> die. Do nothing and death is a surety. Do something and life is a possibility. "Whatsoever he doeth shall prosper... ."[3] *Not whatsoever he wisheth.* Look what happened to and through them when they <u>opted</u> to do something. They were blessed tremendously and through them, the outcasts, an entire city was saved. *Do nothing and not only will you die, we all die – hungry.*

I hear the question, "do what?" *I'm glad you asked.* My answer to you, "I don't know." I have no idea what <u>you,</u> specifically, have been commissioned to do. If you don't know, then I implore you, get in the forward motion of working it out with the Master. I'll tell you what I do know. While you're working through that process, you're going to hit some bumps in the road. *You're gonna get some bumps on the head, too.* But if you take time every now and then to line up the "stuff" with the Word of God, count every trial, situation, promotion, demotion and emotion as "joy", you'll be better for it. Then, practice your praise. Purposely praise so much until you're at a point that without thinking about it, you find yourself in praise. I am convinced that if we, individually, sincerely practice our praise we will see a mightier move of God as a Body. And that's what it's going to take in these last days, a move of God – not a move of flesh.

The Water That Was Made Wine

I don't mind telling you that I have asked God on more than one occasion, "why?" *For as long as I can remember, I've desired to do Your will. Why have you allowed all these bad things to happen in my life?* The more I've tried to live below the radar, the crazier things get and I find myself feeling so exposed. *But God was covering me with His Word* He let me know that He refined me with fire.[4] *Ouch!* It has been necessary for me to become naked and go through situations where only God was able to bring me out. Some doubting Thomases still have to see it to believe it. *I am using you. You are My visual aid.* Although I might have been made a "gazingstock" at times, the "promise" is on the way.[5]

I have taken notice of John 2:7-9.[6] If the

wedding party had not run out of wine, they probably would not have even noticed that Jesus was among them. They were into their thing, having a party. But there was a need that brought Jesus to the center of attention. Most of us, if we didn't have a need every now and then, would not even notice Jesus – what with our parties and all. In looking at this passage, I really wanted to know at what point the miracle occurred. Was it in the pouring in of the water or in the drawing out? How long was the water in the pots? Did Jesus say or do anything in particular to make the change? I've not been able to figure it out. I did see this, though. No one was able to taste the miracle until it was drawn out. If we go through the mess and allow it to just sit there, it is simply mess – stagnant water in a pot. But if we allow the Holy Spirit to draw out of us, that mess becomes not only our message but our miracle. *Thank you Lord, it went in "trouble" and came out "triumph".* Please allow me to "draw out" and share some things I've learned.

Lesson 1: "Let it go". Receive total and complete deliverance from tradition, from the past, - - from *yourself.* Everybody will not be on board with the direction God is leading you. Read my lips and hear me when I scream: Stop trying to drag people where they don't want to go. They *don't* want to go. They <u>not</u> <u>called</u> to go. They <u>can't</u> go. They <u>ain't</u> going. They <u>don't</u> belong there. You will kill yourself trying to drag a bull to the china shop, and all the bull knows to do is tear it up once he gets there. It's not worth it. Release yourself from the mess and others from the stress.

Lesson 2: I am a thermostat and not a thermometer. (*Thank you Dr. Jackson*) I set the atmosphere – the standard. I need not be impressed or intimidated by who's for me or against me. It changes from day to day anyway. Folks *will* pull a Whodini on you. Here today, gone tomorrow. Love 'em when they come. Bless 'em when they leave.

Lesson 3: I had to learn how to fight. My struggles with Darren had been like the face off at the beginning of a boxing match. The enemy and I had been close enough for me to feel his hot breath on my face. His stench was in my nostrils. Going through the struggles of gaining my identity after returning home to a strange place was like sparring with the enemy. We were mostly dancing around. A punch here. A jab there. During my time with Jonathan, in particular, I experienced full fledged warfare. There are at least seven things about fighting that I must never forget.

#1: *Celebrate the victory*. That is correct. First things first. Give God all the praise, glory and honor before, during and after the fight. The louder the better. It confuses the enemy.[7]

#2: *Identify the enemy*. Don't get in the ring and punch the referee. That's not who you are supposed to be fighting. PEOPLE are not my enemies.[8] We must learn to love and accept people right where they are.

#3: *Your adversary, the Devil, does not fight fair*. He will not wait until you are finished being depressed to oppress you. The car engine will not wait until you get the roof fixed before it blows up. It isn't always one thing <u>after</u> another. Sometimes it's one thing <u>on top</u> of another. Adjust your "vision" to   see through the smoke screen. Continue to press toward the mark set in front of you.[9]   *Keep your eyes on the prize.*

#4: Beware of the "bob and weave". The enemy thrives in secrecy and darkness. Expose him. Don't go along with something because "we've always done   it like that" or "that's just how she is." Call it down in the   name of Jesus.[10]

#5: "Watch your head." Guard your thoughts. Think on pure things of God. Don't get caught up in this world's way of thinking. Be

transformed by the renewing of   your   mind. Spiritual warfare – it's all in your mind.[11]

#6: Hold your ground. Having   done   all   to stand, stand therefore. Don't worry about what you <u>don't</u> know. Do what you know.[12]

#7: Chocolate cures all. *Couldn't find a scripture reference, you're just gonna have to trust me on this one.* ☺

I am not suggesting that you don mask and cape and become a demon chaser. Just live Godly. They'll find you. Be ready.

Better or Bitter
I marvel at the awesomeness of my God and am humbled that He continues to reveal different attributes of His character to me.

At the same time, He allows me to see myself over and over again throughout the scriptures. Look at Mary[13]. *Oops, wrong example. I'm not that innocent.* Let's try Ruth[14]. *Missed again. I haven't always been faithful.* What about Esther?[15] *Perish – does that mean I'll miss my hair appointment?* Oh here we go, "a Woman",[16] *There has been "talk"* Leah,[17] *I know what it's like to be rejected.* And Rahab.[18] *Her experiences molded her into a mighty woman of faith, too.*

During a recent personal assessment, I revisited in my mind that tiny Pacific island where I first tasted true Praise and Worship and something amazing occurred to me. During each personal praise service, God and I make a trade off. I give Him my ashes (lingering pain from "stuff") and He gives me beauty. I mourn the dead situations in my life (relationships and finances) and He gives me the oil of joy. I knew Okinawa made a tremendous difference for me but it's taken me all these years to fully realize that I supernaturally disrobed there. I put off the spirit of heaviness and God gave me the spirit of praise.[19] *A mighty God!*

Not all of us gracefully and confidently "step out on faith". Some of us are pushed. I am not concerned right now with how you got where you are. It wasn't my plan to be where I am. Nevertheless, here we are. Too far from where we were to go back but not yet at our divine destination. Stuck...floating somewhere in the middle...this can't be *it*. Just hold on. I refuse to die with treasures still hidden inside me and neither should you. Tread water. Do *some*thing. Don't let the enemy punk you out, man! It ain't *his* call. But how *do* we get there from here? One praise at time. One day at a time. One decision at a time. Why do you keep laying there nursing that broken spirit, holding onto the junk mama 'nem used to do? *There's no stronghold stronger than my God.* Get up! What do you have to lose? After all you've been through – you're still here. Die bitter? If the enemy could kill you, you'd be dead by now. Times awastin'. *The cow's in the corn!* It's within your power - <u>choose</u> to live better. *O'Joy!*

~ ~ ~

Live as right as you can…

…for as long as you can,

you will never <u>become</u> holy.

You just gotta <u>BE</u> holy.[20]

~ ~ ~

Appendix:
Scripture
References

Introduction
1. Deuteronomy 30:19-20

This day I call heaven and earth as witnesses against you that I have set before you life and death, blessings and curses. Now choose life, so that you and your children may live and that you may love the Lord your God, listen to his voice, and hold fast to him. For the Lord is your life, and he will give many years in the land he swore to give to your fathers, Abraham, Isaac and Jacob.

2. James 1:2

Consider it pure joy, my brothers, whenever you face trials of many kind

3. Deuteronomy 23:5

However, the Lord your God would not listen to Balaam but turned the curse into a blessing for you, because the Lord your God loves you.

4. Revelation 12:10-11

Then I heard a loud voice in heaven say: "Now have come the salvation and the power and the kingdom of our God, and the authority of his Christ. For the accuser of our brothers, who accuses them before our God day and night, has been hurled down. They overcame him by the blood of the Lamb and by the word of their testimony; they did not love their lives so much as to shrink from death.

5. Luke 22:31-32

"Simon, Simon, Satan has asked to sift you as wheat. But I have prayed for you, Simon, that your faith may not fail. And when you have turned back, (been converted) strengthen your brothers."

6. Joshua 4:20-24

And Joshua set up at Gilgal the twelve stones they had taken out of the Jordan. He said to the Israelites. "In the future when your descendants ask their fathers, 'What do these stones mean?' tell them, 'Israel crossed the Jordan on dry ground.' For the Lord your God dried up the Jordan before you until you had crossed over. The Lord your God did to the Jordan just what he had done to the Red Sea when he dried it up before us until we had crossed over. He did this so that all the peoples of the earth might know that the hand of the Lord is powerful and so that you might always fear the Lord your God.

Chapter 1: Just Who Do You Think You Are?
1. Proverbs 31:10-31

A wife of noble character who can find? She is worth far more than rubies. Her husband has full confidence in her and lacks nothing of value. She brings him good, not harm, all the days of her life. She selects wool and flax and works with eager hands. She is like the merchant ships, bringing her food from afar. She gets up while it is still dark; she provides food for her family and portions for her servant girls. She considers a field and buys it; out of her earnings she plants a vineyard. She sets about her work vigorously; her arms are strong for her tasks. She sees that her trading is profitable, and her lamp does not go out at night. In her hand she holds the distaff and grasps the spindle with her fingers. She opens her arms to the poor and extends her hands to the needy. When it snows, she has no fear for her household; for all of them are clothed in scarlet. She makes coverings for her bed; she is clothed in fine linen and purple. Her husband is respected at the city gate, where he takes his seat among the elders of the land. She makes linen garments and sells them, and supplies the merchants with sashes. She is clothed with strength and dignity; she can laugh at the days to come. She speaks with wisdom, and faithful instruction is on her tongue. She watches over the affairs of her household and does not eat the bread of idleness. Her children arise and call her blessed; her husband also, and he praises her. Many women do noble things, but you surpass them all. Charm is deceptive, and beauty is fleeting; but a woman who fears the Lord is to be praised. Give her the reward she has earned, and let her works bring her praise at the city gate.

2. Acts 3:1-2
One day Peter and John were going up to the temple at the time of prayer – at three in the afternoon. Now a man crippled from birth was being carried to the temple gate called Beautiful, where he was put every day to beg from those going into the temple courts.

3. Amos 3:3
Do two walk together, unless they have agreed to do so?

4. Ephesians 6:12
For our struggle is not against flesh and blood, but against the rulers, against the authorities, against the powers of this dark world and

against the spiritual forces of evil in the heavenly realms.

5. Genesis 2:21-3:7

So the Lord God caused the man to fall into a deep sleep; and while he was sleeping, he took one of the man's ribs and closed up the place with flesh. Then the Lord God made a woman from the rib he had taken out of the man, and he brought her to the man. The man said, "This is now bone of my bones and flesh of my flesh; she shall be called 'woman' for she was taken out of man." For this reason a man will leave his father and mother and be united to his wife, and they will become one flesh. The man and his wife were both naked, and they felt no shame. Now the serpent was more crafty than any of the wild animals the Lord God had made. He said to the woman, "Did God really say, 'You must not eat from any tree in the garden'?" The woman said to the serpent, "We may eat fruit from the trees in the garden, but God did say, 'You must not eat fruit from the tree that is in the middle of the garden, and you must not touch it, or you will die.'" "You will not surely die," the serpent said to the woman. For God knows that when you eat of it your eyes will be opened, and you will be like

God, knowing good and evil." When the woman saw that the fruit of the tree was good for food and pleasing to the eye, and also desirable for gaining wisdom, she took some and ate it. She also gave some to her husband, who was with her, and he ate it. Then the eyes of both of them were opened, and they realized they were naked; so they sewed fig leaves together and made coverings for themselves.

6. Genesis 3:20
Adam named his wife Eve, because she would become the mother of all the living.

7. Genesis 29:25
When morning came, there was Leah! So Jacob said to Laban, "What is this you have done to me? I served you for Rachel, didn't I? Why have you deceived me?"

8. Genesis 3:20 (See reference #6)

9. Genesis 29:35
She conceived again, and when she gave birth to a son she said, "This time I will praise the Lord," So she named him Judah. Then she stopped having children.

10. Luke 3:23-33

Now Jesus himself was about thirty years old when he began his ministry. He was the son, so it was thought, of Joseph, the son of Heli, the son of Matthat, the son of Levi, the son of Melchi, the son of Jan'na-i, the son of Joseph, the son of Mattathi'as, the son of Amos, the son of Nahum, the son of Esli, the son of Nag'ga-i, the son of Ma'ath, the son of Mattathi'as, the son of Sem'e-in, the son of Josech, the son of Joda, the son of Jo-an'an, the son of Rhesa, the son of Zerub'babel, the son of She-al'ti-el, the son of Neri, the son of Melchi, the son of Addi, the son of Cosam, the son of Elma'dam, the son of Er, the son of Joshua, the son of Elie'zer, the son of Jorim, the son of Matthat, the son of Levi, the son of Simeon, the son of Judah, the son of Joseph, the son of Jonam, the   son of Eli'akim, [31] the son of Me'le-a, the son of Menna, the son of Mat'tatha, the son of Nathan, the son of David, the son of Jesse, the son of Obed, the son of Bo'az, the son of Sala, the son of Nahshon, the son of Ammin'adab, the son of Admin, the son of Arni, the son of Hezron, the son of Perez, the son of Judah.

11. 1 Corinthians 2:9
However, as it is written: "No eye has seen, no

ear has heard, no mind has conceived what God has prepared for those who love him."

Chapter 2: There's No Place Like Home
1. John 12:32
But I, when I am lifted up from the earth, will draw all men to myself."

2. 1 Corinthians 15:31
I die every day – I mean that, brothers – just as surely as I glory over you in Christ Jesus our Lord.

3. I Samuel 15:11, 22-23, 27, 35
I am grieved that I have made Saul king because he has turned away from me and has not carried out my instructions. So Samuel was troubled and he cried out to the Lord all that night.

But Samuel replied: "Does the Lord delight in burnt offerings and sacrifices as much as in obeying the voice of the Lord? To obey is better than sacrifice, and to heed is better than the fat of rams. For rebellion is like the sin of divination (witchcraft), and arrogance like the evil of idolatry. Because you have rejected the word of the Lord, he has rejected you as king."

As Samuel turned to leave, Saul caught hold of the hem of his robe, and it tore.

Until the day Samuel died, he did not go to see Saul again, though Samuel mourned for him. And the Lord was grieved that he had made Saul king over Israel.

4. 1 Samuel 16:14
Now the spirit of the Lord had departed from Saul and an evil spirit form the Lord tormented him.

5. I Samuel 18:10-11
The next day an evil spirit from God came forcefully upon Saul. He was prophesying in his house, while David was playing the harp, as he usually did. Saul had a spear in his hand and hurled it, saying to himself, "I'll pin David to the wall." But David eluded him twice.

6. Psalm 55:12-14
If an enemy were insulting me, I could endure it; if a foe were raising himself against me, I could hide from him, But it is you, a man like myself, my companion, my close friend, with whom I once enjoyed sweet fellowship as we walked with the throng at the house of God.

7. Isaiah 6:1,8

In the year that King Uzziah died, I saw the Lord seated on a throne, high and exalted, and the train of his robe filled the temple.

Then I heard the voice of the Lord saying, "Whom shall I send? And who will go for us?" And I said, "Here am I. Send me!"

8. Matthew 16:13

When Jesus came to the region of Caesarea Philippi, he asked his disciples, "Who do people say the Son of Man is?"

9. Mark 14:3-4

While he was in Bethany, reclining at the table in the home of a man known as Simon the Leper, a woman came with   an alabaster jar of very expensive perfume made of pure nard. She broke the jar and poured the perfume on his head. Some of those present were saying indignantly to one another, "Why this waste of perfume?"

10. John 1:11

He came to that which was his own, but his own did not receive him.

Chapter 3: When A Lie Becomes The Truth
1. Judges 16:1, 14-20
One day Samson went to Gaza where he saw a prostitute. He went in to spend the night with her.

So while he was sleeping, Delilah took the seven braids of his head, wove them into the fabric and tightened it with the pin. Again she called to him, "Samson, the Philistines are upon you!" He awoke from his sleep and pulled up the pin and the loom with the fabric. Then she said to him, "How can you say 'I love you,' when you won't confide in me? This is the third time you have made a fool of me and haven't told me the secret of your great strength." With such nagging she prodded him day after day until he was tired to death. So he told her everything. "No razor has ever been used on my head," he said, "Because I have been a Nazirite set apart to God since birth. If my head were shaved, my strength would leave me, and I would become as weak as any other man." When she saw that he had told her everything, she sent word to the rulers of the Philistines, "Come back once more, he has told me everything." So the rulers of the Philistines returned with the silver in their hands. Having put him to sleep on her lap, she called a man to shave off the seven braids of his hair and so began to subdue him. And his strength left him. Then she called, "Samson, the Philistines are upon you!" He awoke from his sleep and thought, "I'll go out as before and shake myself free." But he did not know that the Lord had left him.

2. Luke 24:1-8

On the first day of the week, very early in the morning, the women took the spices they had prepared and went to the tomb. They found the stone rolled away from the tomb, but when they entered they did not find the body of the Lord Jesus. While they were wondering about this, suddenly two men in clothes that gleamed like lightning stood beside them. In their fright the women bowed down with their faces to the ground, but the men said to them, "Why do you look for the living among the dead? He is not here; he has risen! Remember how he told you, while he was still with you in Galilee: 'The Son of Man must be delivered into the hands of sinful men, be crucified and on the third day be raised again.'"

3. Revelation 22:7
(Open Bible® Study Edition copyright © 1990 by Thomas Nelson, Inc)
Behold, I come quickly: Blessed is he that keepeth the sayings of the prophecy of this book.

4. 2 Corinthians 5:17
Therefore, if anyone is in Christ, he is a new creation; the old has gone, the new has come!

5. 2 Corinthians 10:4
The weapons we fight with are not the weapons of the world. On the contrary, they have divine power to demolish strongholds.

6. Philippians 4:6
Do not be anxious about anything, but in everything, by prayer and petition, with thanksgiving, present your requests to God.

7. Galatians 3:26-29
You are all sons of God through faith in Christ Jesus, for all of you who were baptized into Christ have clothed yourselves with Christ. There is neither Jew nor Greek, slave nor free, male nor female, for you are all one in Christ Jesus. If you belong to Christ, then you are Abraham's seed, and heirs according to the promise.

8. Exodus 12:12-13

On that same night I will pass through Egypt and strike down every first-born – both men and animals – and I will bring judgment on all the gods of Egypt. I am the Lord. The blood will be a sign for you on the houses where you are; and when I see the blood, I will pass over you. No destructive plague will touch you when I strike Egypt.

9. 1 Peter 1:18-19

For you know that it was not with perishable things such as silver or gold that you were redeemed from the empty way of life handed down to you from your forefathers, but with the precious blood of Christ, a lamb without blemish or defect.

10. Philippians 4:8

Finally, brothers, whatever is true, whatever is noble, whatever is right, whatever is admirable – if anything is excellent or praiseworthy – think about such things.

11. 2 Samuel 9:1-3,6

David asked, "Is there anyone still left of the house of Saul to whom I can show kindness for

Jonathan's sake?" Now there was a servant of Saul's household named Ziba. They called him to appear before David, and the king said to him, "Are you Ziba?" "Your servant," he replied. The king asked, "Is there no one still left of the house of Saul to whom I can show God's kindness?" Ziba answered the king, "There is still a son of Jonathan: he is crippled in both feet."

When Mephibosheth son of Jonathan, the son of Saul, came to David, he bowed down to pay him honor. David said, "Mephibosheth!" "Your servant," he replied.

12. 2 Timothy 3:5
Having a form of godliness but denying its power. Have nothing to do with them.

13. 2 Samuel 4:4
Jonathan, son of Saul, had a son who was lame in both feet. He was five years old when the news about Saul and Jonathan came from Jezreel. His nurse picked him up and fled, but as she hurried to leave, he fell to leave, and became crippled. His name was Mephibosheth.

14. 2 Samuel 9:6-7

When Mephibosheth, son of Jonathan, the son of Saul, came to David, he bowed down to pay him honor. David said, "Mephibosheth!" "Your servant," he replied. "Don't be afraid," David said to him, "for I will surely show you kindness for the sake of your father Jonathan. I will restore you all the land that belonged to your grandfather Saul and you will always eat at my table.

15. James 3:9-10

With the tongue we praise our Lord and Father, and with it we curse men, who have been made in God's likeness. Out of the same mouth come praise and cursing. My brothers, this should not be.

16. James 1:14

But each one is tempted when, by his own evil desire, he is dragged away and enticed.

17. Psalm 34:19

A righteous man may have many troubles, but the Lord delivers him from them all.

18. 2 Peter 2:1-3

But there were also false prophets among the

people, just as there will be false teachers among you. They will secretly introduce destructive heresies, even denying the sovereign Lord who bought them – bringing swift destruction on themselves. Many will follow their shameful ways and will bring the way of truth into disrepute. In their greed these teachers will exploit you with stories they have made up. Their condemnation has long been hanging over them and their destruction has not been sleeping.

19. Romans 1:26-27
Because of this God gave them over to shameful lusts. Even their women exchanged natural relations for unnatural ones. In the same way the men also abandoned natural relations with women and were inflamed with lust for one another. Men committed indecent acts with other men, and received in themselves the due penalty for their perversion.

20. 2 Peter 2:10
This is especially true of those who follow the corrupt desire of the sinful nature and despise authority. Bold and arrogant, these men are not afraid to slander celestial beings.

21.2 Timothy 3:3b

…not lovers of the good.

22. 2 Timothy 3:8-9

Just as Jannes and Jambres opposed Moses, so also these men oppose the truth – men of depraved minds, who as far as the faith is concerned, are rejected. But they will not get very far because, as in the case of those men, their folly will be clear to everyone.

23. Psalm 35:11

Ruthless witnesses come forward; they question me on things I know nothing about.

24. Psalm 37:32

The wicked lie in wait for the righteous, seeking their very lives.

25. 2 Peter 2:9

Then the Lord knows how to rescue godly men from trials and to hold the unrighteous for the day of judgment, while continuing their punishment.

26. Matthew 27:35

When they had crucified him, they divided up his clothes by casting lots.

27. Psalm 54

Save me, O God, by your name; vindicate me by your might. Hear my prayer, O God; listen to the words of my mouth. Strangers are attacking me; ruthless men seek my life – men without regard for God. Surely God is my help; the Lord is the one who sustains me. Let evil recoil on those who slander me; in your faithfulness destroy them. I will sacrifice a freewill offering to you; I will praise your name, O Lord, for it is good. For he has delivered me from all my troubles, and my eyes have looked in triumph on my foes.

28. Hosea 1:2
When the Lord began to speak through Hosea, the Lord said to him, "Go take to yourself an adulterous wife and children of unfaithfulness, because the land is guilty of the vilest adultery in departing from the Lord."

29. Revelation 12:10-14
Then I heard a loud voice in heaven say: "Now have come the salvation and the power and the kingdom of our God, and the authority of his Christ. For the accuser of our brothers, who accuses them before our God day and night, has been hurled down. The overcame him by the blood of the Lamb and by the word of their

testimony; they did not love their lives so much as to shrink from death. Therefore rejoice, you heavens and you will dwell in them! But woe to the earth and the sea, because the devil has gone down to you! He is filled with fury because he knows that his time is short." When the dragon saw that he had been hurled to the earth, he pursued the woman who had given birth to the male child. The woman was given the two wings of a great eagle, so that she might fly to the place prepared for her in the desert, where she would be taken care of for a time, times and half a time, out of the serpent's reach.

Chapter 4: Better or Bitter
1. James 1:2
Consider it pure joy, my brothers, whenever you face trials of many kinds.

2. 2 Kings 7:3-16
Now there were four men with leprosy at the entrance of the city gate. They said to each other, "Why stay here until we die? If we say, 'We'll go into the city' – the famine is there, and we will die. And if we stay here, we will die. So let's go over to the camp of the

Arameans and surrender. If they spare us, we live; if they kill us, then we die." At dusk they got up and went to the camp of the Arameans. When they reached the edge of the camp, not a man was there, for the Lord had caused the Arameans to hear the sound of chariots and horses and a great army, so that they said to one another, "Look, the king of Israel has hired the Hittite and Egyptian kings to attack us! So they got up and fled in the dusk and abandoned their tents and their horses and donkeys. They left the camp as it was and ran for their lives. The men who had leprosy reached the edge of the camps and entered one of the tents. They ate and drank and carried away silver, gold and clothes and went off and hid them. They returned and entered another tent and took some things from it and hid them also. Then they said to each other, "We're not doing right. This is a day of good news and we are keeping it to ourselves. If we wait until daylight, punishment will overtake us. Let's go at once and report this to the royal palace." So they went and called out to the city gatekeepers and told them, "We went into the Aramean camp and not a man was there – not a sound of anyone – only tethered horses and donkeys and the tents left just as they were." The gatekeepers shouted the news and it was reported within th palace. The kings got up in the night and said to his officers, "I will tell you what the Arameans have done to us. They know we are starving so they have left the camp to hide in the countryside, thinking, 'They will surely come out and then we will take them alive and get into the city.'" One of his officers answered, "Have some men take five of the horses that are left in the city. Their plight will be like that of all the Israelites left here – yes, they will only be like all these Israelites who are doomed. So let us send them to find out what happened." So they selected two chariots with their horses, and the king sent them after the Aramean army. He commanded the drivers, "Go and find out what has happened." They followed them as far as the Jordan and they found the whole road strewn with the clothing and equipment the Arameans had thrown away in their headlong flight. So the messengers returned and reported to the king. Then the people went out and plundered the camp of the Armeans.

3. Psalm 1:3

He is like a tree planted by streams of water, which yields its fruit in season and whose leaf does not wither. Whatever he does prospers.

4. Isaiah 48:10
See, I have refined you, though not as silver; I have tested you   in the furnace of affliction.

5. Hebrews 10:31-36
It is a dreadful thing to fall into the hands of the living God. Remember those earlier days after you had received the light, when you stood your ground in great contest in the face of suffering.   Sometimes you were publicly exposed to insult and persecution; at other times you stood side by side with those who were so treated. You sympathized with those in prison and joyfully accepted the confiscation of your property, because you knew that you yourselves had better and lasting possessions. So do not throw away your confidence; it will be richly rewarded. You need to persevere so that when you have done the will of God, you will receive what he has promised.

6. John 2:7-10
Jesus said to the servants, "Fill the jars with water," so they filled them to the brim. Then he told them, "Now draw some out and take it to the master of the banquet." They did so, and

the master of the banquet tasted the water that had been turned into wine. He did not realize where it had come from, though the servants who had been drawn the water knew. Then he called the bridegroom aside and said, "Everyone brings out the choice wine first and then the cheaper wine after the guests have had too much to drink, but you have saved the best till now."

7. Judges 7:17-21

"Watch me," he told them. "Follow my lead. When I get to the edge of the camp, do exactly as I do. When I and all who are with me blow our trumpets, then from all around the camp blow yours and shout, 'For the Lord and for Gideon.'" Gideon and the hundred men with him reached the edge of the camp at the beginning of the middle watch, just after they had changed the guard. They blew their trumpets and broke the jars that were in their hands. The three companies blew the trumpets and smashed the jars. Grasping the torches in their left hands and holding in their right hands the trumpets they were to blow, they shouted, "A sword for the Lord and for Gideon!" While each man held his position around the camp, all the Midianites ran, crying out as they fled.

8. Ephesians 6:12

For our struggle is not against flesh and blood, but against the rulers, against the authorities, against the powers of this dark world and against the spiritual forces of evil in the heavenly realms.

9. Philippians 3:14

I press on toward the goal to win the prize for which God has called me heavenward in Christ Jesus.

10. John 3:19-20

This is the verdict; Light has come into the world, but men loved darkness instead of light because their deeds were evil. Everyone who does evil hates the light, and will not come into the light for fear that his deeds will be exposed.

11. Philippians 4:8

Finally, brothers, whatever is true, whatever is noble, whatever is right, whatever is pure, whatever is lovely, whatever is admirable – if anything is excellent or praiseworthy – think about such things.

12. Ephesians 6:13-14

Therefore put on the full armor of God, so that when the day of evil comes you may be able to stand your ground, and after you have done everything to stand. Stand firm then, with the belt of truth buckled around your waist, with the breastplate of righteousness in place.

13. Luke 1:27
To a virgin pledged to be married to a man named Joseph, a descendant of David. The virgin's name was Mary.

14. Ruth 1:16-17
But Ruth replied, "Don't urge me to leave you or to turn back from you. Where you go I will go and where you stay I will stay. Your people will be my people and your God my God. Where you die I will die and there I will be buried. May the Lord deal with me, be it ever so severely if anything but death separates you and me."

15. Esther 4:16
Go, gather together all the Jews who are in Susa, and fast for me. Do not eat or drink for three days, night or day. I and my maids will

fast as you do. When this is done, I will go to the king, even though it is against the law. And if I perish, I perish.

16. Mark 14:3-5
While he was in Bethany, reclining at the table in the home of a man known as Simon the Leper, a woman came with an alabaster jar of very expensive perfume, made of pure nard. She broke the jar and poured the perfume on his head. Some of those present were saying indignantly to one another, "Why this waste of perfume? It could have been sold for more than a year's wages and the money given to the poor." And they rebuked her harshly.

17. Genesis 29:30-31
Jacob lay with Rachel also, and he loved Rachel more than Leah. And he worked for Laban another seven years. When the Lord saw that Leah was not loved, he opened her womb, but Rachel was barren.

18. Joshua 2:1, 8-15
Then Joshua son of Nun secretly sent two spies from Shittim. "Go, look over the land," he said, "especially Jericho." So they went and entered

the house of a prostitute named Rahab and stayed there.

Before the spies lay down for the night, she went up on the roof and said to them, "I know that the Lord has given this land to you and that a great fear of you has fallen on us, so that all who live in this country are melting in fear because of you. We have heard how the Lord dried up the water of the Red Sea for you when you came out of Egypt, and what you did to Sihon and Og, the two kings of the Amorites east of the Jordan whom you completely destroyed. When we heard of it, our hearts melted and everyone's courage failed because of you, for the Lord your God is God in heaven above and on the earth below. Now, then, please swear to me by the Lord that you will show kindness to my family, because I have shown kindness to you. Give me a sure sign that you will spare the lives of my father and mother, my brothers and sisters, and all who belong to them and that you will save us from death." "Our lives for you lives!" the men assured her. "If you don't tell what we are doing, we will treat you kindly and faithfully when the Lord gives us the land." So she let them down by a rope through the window, for the house she lived in was part of the city wall.

19. Isaiah 61:3
To provide for those who grieve in Zion – to bestow on them a crown of beauty instead of ashes, the oil of gladness instead of mourning, and a garment of praise instead of a spirit of despair.   They will be called oaks of righteousness, a planting of the Lord for the display of his splendor.

20. 1 Peter 1:14-16
As obedient children, do not conform to the evil desires you had when you lived in ignorance.   But just as he who called you is holy, so be holy in all you do; for it is written: "Be holy, because I am holy."

Made in the USA
Columbia, SC
14 December 2024

48054391R00115